Penguin Education

Penguin Modern Economics Texts
General Editor: B. J. McCormick

Microeconomics
Editor: B. J. McCormick

The Theory of Taxation
Charles M. Allan

The Theory of Taxation

Charles M. Allan

Penguin Books

Penguin Books Ltd, Harmondsworth,
Middlesex, England
Penguin Books Inc., 7110 Ambassador Road,
Baltimore, Md 21207, U.S.A.
Penguin Books Australia Ltd,
Ringwood, Victoria, Australia

First published 1971
Copyright © Charles M. Allan, 1971

Made and printed in Great Britain by
C. Nicholls & Company Ltd, Manchester
Set in Monotype Times

Penguin Modern Economics Texts

This volume is one in a series of unit texts designed to reduce the price of knowledge for students of economics in universities and colleges of higher education. The units may be used singly or in combination with other units to form attractive and unusual teaching programmes. The volumes will cover the major teaching areas but they will differ from conventional books in their attempt to chart and explore new directions in economic thinking. The traditional divisions of theory and applied, of positive and normative and of micro and macro will tend to be blurred as authors impose new and arresting ideas on the traditional corpus of economics. Some units will fall into conventional patterns of thought but many will transgress established beliefs.

Penguin Modern Economics Texts are published in units in order to achieve certain objectives. First, a large range of short texts at inexpensive prices gives the teacher flexibility in planning his course and recommending texts for it. Secondly, the pace at which important new work is published requires the project to be adaptable. Our plan allows a unit to be revised or a fresh unit to be added with maximum speed and minimal cost to the reader.

The international range of authorship will, it is hoped, bring out the richness and diversity in economic analysis and thinking.

B. J. MCC.

Contents

Editorial Foreword

Taxation is concerned with two problems. First, how to finance the provision of those goods – defence, law and order are examples – which a market economy cannot easily provide: call them public or collective goods. Second, to finance those programmes which will eliminate the side effects of a market economy – poverty, unemployment, urban blight and atmospheric pollution: these are the public bads, usually discussed in social economics. Goods and bads both arise because of deficiencies in the system of ownership rights in a private enterprise economy. If I build a beautiful house someone else has a pleasant view. If I do not possess the skills to earn a living wage who should I blame for my genetic make-up? The imperfect market in parents? And there can never be a once-and-for-all resolution of goods and bads since these depend upon the changes thrown up by the hierarchy of wants. Which is how tax problems are always with us.

Many economists have investigated the problems surrounding taxation and the merit of Mr Allan's book is that it provides a lucid and pleasant commentary on both personalities and problems. He shows how the deficiencies of the market lead to a demand of state provision of goods and services. But he carefully points out that we must not always expect those who benefit from state action to pay for such benefits. We should not expect the poor to pay for their state-provided housing. Indeed he observes the current thinking which suggests that the rich may benefit from income redistribution and that in order to ensure their benefit the rich may insist upon redistribution in kind rather than cash.

Somehow the various goods that people want but cannot obtain in a market economy must be provided. A tax base must be found. As Mr Allan demonstrates there are many bases for taxation, each of which has associated disadvantages. Unfortunately we know nothing about the empirical nature of the trade-offs involved in various tax regimes. Mr Allan does however provide some wisdom in an area riddled with fossilized tax structures, myths and prejudices.

B.J.MCC.

Part One

Chapter 1 describes how the need for government activity and
so for taxation arises. Chapter 2 defines, lists and
classifies the fiscal alternatives available to governments
and introduces the terminology of tax analysis. In
Chapter 3 the various aspects of efficiency of taxes are
described. Chapter 4 tackles the problem of incidence;
of identifying the final taxpayers. For example, the
question as to whether companies are the real payers of
corporation tax or whether they simply pass the tax
burden on to their customers in the form of higher
prices is investigated. Chapter 5 looks briefly at the vexing
question of incentives.

1 How the Need for Taxation Arises

The perfectly competitive economy appears, at first sight at least, capable of functioning in a highly satisfactory way without formal government and so without taxation. In perfect competition the problems of production, distribution and exchange are solved by the free actions of free men pursuing their personal desires in free markets. Capitalists try to make as big profits as they can but cannot exploit. If they produce shoddy goods, produce inefficiently so that prices are too high, or try to profiteer, the goods will not sell and the consumers will turn to the goods of other manufacturers. Workers try to get the best pay and conditions that they can, but they cannot get more than the value of what they can produce for if they did it would profit the employer to sack them. And they cannot get much less than the value of what they produce for then it would pay another capitalist to employ them at slightly higher wage rates. Exchange is always fair in free markets because each party to a transaction must benefit or else he would refuse to deal.

When one looks at Western economies this stylized market system seems fairly credible as an approximation of what would happen if state intervention were abolished. One can imagine most consumer goods being produced without state intervention. As the demand for new products developed, so new entrepreneurs would arise to profit by producing them. As consumer demand changed, the enterprises which produced for declining markets would start to make losses. Automatically they would disappear or change their functions.

Why then, when we have this self-regulating machinery for producing the goods we require, do we have the huge apparatus which comprises the public sector and whose gross current expenditure in 1968 was equal to some 35 per cent of

United States and 45 per cent of British Gross Domestic Product?

The answer will be given in three parts. Firstly, the government provides social goods and merit goods because some of these goods have characteristics which make them less suitable for market provision. Secondly, the government spends money on supporting the poor. And thirdly, the government takes steps to make up for certain failures of the market to act successfully as a planning mechanism.

Social goods and merit goods

The market operates on two principles:

1. *The exclusion principle*. This simply states that those who do not pay the market price for goods are excluded from their consumption.

2. *Revealed preference*. The market operates on information provided by consumers' buying habits at going prices. People are willing to reveal their preferences because they will be excluded from consumption if they do not.

Revealed preference and the exclusion principle work well in ordering the production, distribution and exchange of most goods and services. But there are goods for which preferences will not be fully revealed and to which the exclusion principle cannot be applied effectively, and which will not be provided in a satisfactory way in a market economy. These are social goods and merit goods. We shall introduce these concepts by way of a consideration of three characteristics which all goods and services have in some measure.

Firstly, there is the *competitiveness* or *jointness* of the consumption for which the good is produced. Thus sweets are consumed competitively because if one man eats a sweet no one else can eat that sweet. The more sweets one person eats the fewer there are left for others. On the other hand, street lighting is consumed jointly. The more street lighting one person gets the more street lighting everyone in that street gets.

Secondly, the costs and benefits of the production and consumption of a good may either be *internal*, in which case they will be enjoyed exclusively by the producers and consumers of that good, or they may be *external*, in which case benefits and/or costs will be borne by third parties. If I let my house fall into disrepair or disrepute I will suffer an internal loss in the fall in my property values. But my neighbours will suffer an external loss in so far as my disreputable behaviour brings down the property values of my neighbourhood. If I am protected by vaccination from an infectious disease it is an internal benefit to me. But I also confer external benefits on all others with whom I come in contact because I am now less likely to infect them. So the extent of the externalities (they may be called spillovers, social costs and benefits or neighbourhood effects) is an important attribute of goods and services.

And thirdly, there is the question of ignorance. The consumer is faced with a very large range of goods and services upon which to spend his income. Most goods give rise to a fairly easily comprehensible set of benefits, e.g. coal keeps people warm, cars transport people, and carpets help to drown the noise of children. We can expect people to make rational choices between such goods. But there are other benefits which are less easily comprehended for a variety of reasons.

1. Ignorance may arise from the separation in time of cost and benefit. Medical insurance has to be taken out when one is fit, and it may be easy for a fit person to underestimate the probability or the extent of illness.

2. The nature of the benefits may not be understood. Oranges and apples both taste good, but the benefits to health which accrue to consumers of these fruits almost all come from the orange.

3. In the case of education, payment is made by parents and the benefits enjoyed by the children, so that even if the benefits are understood the ultimate consumer is not in a position to pay for his education until after he has consumed it.

The market as a mechanism for giving people what will make them happiest does not work well if there is much ignorance, because if people do not know the true costs and benefits they cannot choose rationally. Nor can the market cope with those externalities because they may affect neither party to economic activity. And if there is jointness the market will be frustrated by 'free-riders' who refuse to reveal their preferences for joint consumption goods because they cannot be excluded from the consumption of other people's.

Table 1
Characteristics of Goods and Services

Market provision	State provision
1. Private costs and benefits	1. Externalities
2. Competitive consumption	2. Joint consumption
3. Knowledge	3. Ignorance
(a) Payment and benefit simultaneous	(a) Payment and benefit not simultaneous
(b) Benefits obvious	(b) Benefits obscure
(c) Payee and beneficiary identical	(c) Payee and beneficiary non-identical

These characteristics of goods are listed in Table 1. Those which make for successful market provision are on the left and those which tend to favour state provision are on the right. It is important to realize that, for example, most goods which give rise mainly to private benefits will have some associated externalities and that the costs and benefits of all consumption are to *some* extent obscure. However, the more the characteristics of goods are like those in the right hand column, i.e. appropriate state provision, the less likely it is that market provision will be optimal.

Social goods are goods which are provided by the state principally because of the jointness of their consumption. These include defence, law and order, light, housing, public beach clearance and urban parks. The state must provide these since the exclusion principle cannot be applied. If one person in a country is defended from invasion so is everyone else; there is thus absolute jointness.

Merit goods are goods which are provided by the state mainly because of ignorance and externalities. Such merit goods are education, health services and orange juice. The benefits of orange juice to the health of the young are not widely understood and fizzy lemonade will often be preferred on grounds of taste. And the choice of an optimum amount of education may be too difficult for many people for the reasons mentioned on page 15. And even if the private benefits are understood the external benefits, the benefits accruing to society as a whole as a result of literacy and numeracy which Lord Robbins (1964) found so important, cannot be taken into account in a market economy.

Merit goods are under-consumed in a free market because of ignorance and externalities. *Demerit* goods are over-consumed because of ignorance or externalities, and the government steps in to discourage consumption of such goods. Cigarettes give external diseconomies of air pollution, and the separation in time between the enjoyment of smoking and possibility of cancer or bronchitis may make for ignorant decisions. The government may discourage consumption of demerit goods by taxation or legislation.

Part of chapter 8 will be devoted to a discussion of some of the problems and arguments advanced in the political economy of how much social and merit goods should be provided by the state. There is great disagreement on the extent to which such state intervention is necessary, but general agreement that the state must provide the social goods law and order and defence to keep invasion, theft, sharp practice and assassination down to levels which allow the market economy to function smoothly. These government expenditures give rise to the need for taxation.

Income redistribution

The second category of government expenditure which adds to the need for taxation includes all attempts to raise the share of the National Income going to the poor. In a purely market economy all income would be distributed in accordance with the contribution of output of each individual or each individual's assets. This could leave a large section of the population destitute, e.g. those who through mental, physical or temperamental accident do not make much or any contribution to output and whose parents did not provide a legacy of productive assets. There are disputes about the level of provision for the poor but general agreement that this is a proper function of government in the pursuit of social welfare.

Redistributive expenditures may be either in kind or in cash. The universal provision of social goods, the universal provision of certain merit goods and the provision of other merit goods selectively in favour of the poor or in such a way as to make it unlikely that richer people will use such goods, and the provision or subsidization of private goods such as basic food-stuffs, all imply subsidies in kind. Or redistributive expenditures may take the form of cash payments to the old, the sick and the inept, usually in some proportion to family size.

Other market imperfections

There is another source of government expenditure which although they may be described as social goods deserve a section to themselves. The market imperfections referred to here provide a reason for government intervention arising out of the failure of the market as a planning mechanism, rather than out of the nature of the goods and services in question.

Free markets may give rise to *monopolies* whose function it is to raise prices by restricting output. This provides reason for state expenditure on anti-trust activity.

On the other hand, free markets may give rise to *wasteful competition*. Road and rail transport provide examples. The waste involved in competing firms operating parallel rails or roads is likely to be great. So the state may have to enforce and control monopolization or nationalize such services to promote efficiency.

Then the market may fall down as a device for *locational planning*. Two examples will illustrate this point. Figure 1 shows a street served by two fruit-barrow boys. All their customers live in the street and are evenly dispersed along it. The ideal location, from both barrow boys' and consumers' point of view, will be as in Figure 1(a). Then each will get half the trade and no consumer will have to walk more than a quarter of the length of the street. But if there is no collaboration and no state planning, both barrow boys will locate themselves as in Figure 1(d). This will not suit the consumers, half of whom will have to walk further to get their fruit. It will not suit the barrow boys either as some consumers will not find the extra walk worthwhile.

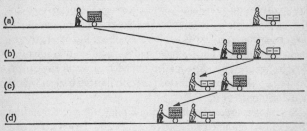

Figure 1

Similarly the location of odorous factories in residential areas is likely unless there is non-market locational planning. A special case where uncontrolled private enterprise may lead to location which is incompatible with the public interest was provided by an Aberdeen laundry. This was centrally located, which was convenient both for customers and for workers. But this laundry produced foul smoke pollution which, while unpleasant for all, actually increased the trade of the laundry by dirtying people's clothing.

Governments often involve themselves in expenditures designed to *accelerate the rate of growth* which would obtain in a free market. This may be justified because of the ignorance of investors of the value of future income or of the ability of compound interest to solve problems of poverty, or because of the insufficiency of investment in free markets as the external benefits of learning are not taken into account by investors, or because the other market imperfections inhibit growth.

And lastly there is the question of *stabilization*. Capitalist systems have shown themselves prone to market imperfections in the form of trade cycles, i.e. successive periods of inflation and unemployment. Governments provide machinery for smoothing out such cycles to avoid inflation and unemployment.

Stabilization policy and monetary theory

The provision of social goods, merit goods and support for the poor implies the use by the public sector of a proportion of the National Product. In pre-Keynesian times the primary function of taxation was to finance these government expenditures. Taxation was levied so as to exactly balance intended government expenditure. The classical budget required that intended government revenue R_g equalled intended government expenditure E_g year by year. The classical or balanced budget was in equilibrium when $R_g = E_g$.

Since taxes are normally paid in money, the pre-Keynesian theory also contained a theory of money and the workings of a monetary economy. Despite the ample evidence to the contrary, unemployment was deemed to be a non-equilibrium state of affairs. The natural order was one of full employment and an unfortunate consequence of this was a failure on the part of economists to find a solution in macroeconomics to the problems of mass unemployment in the 1930s. The conclusion that market economies would tend to full employment was predicated on two assumptions which were not reflective of the real world. The first of these was the assumption that wages would be flexible downwards so that during depressions wages and prices would fall. This would raise the real value of people's savings. They would then feel richer and so spend more – thereby raising employment. The second assumption was that a flexible rate of interest would effectively equate the amount people saved with the amount others intended to invest.

In such a world a pound removed from the private sector would reduce investment and consumption by exactly one pound, so that one pound's worth of goods and services no more and no less would be freed for government use. To maintain this full employment it was clear that the budget had to balance.

However, the automatic tendency of aggregate demand and

aggregate supply to equate at the full-employment level was denied by Keynes (1936). Hence a second major requirement of fiscal policy became to correct for any excess or deficiency of aggregate demand. This would in all but a special case require an unbalancing of the budget, producing either surpluses or deficits as the state of demand and the availability of resources required. Keynes's principal remedy for mass unemployment was a great increase in government expenditure quite unaccompanied by tax increases.

The Keynesian budget does not seek to balance revenue and expenditure but seeks to induce a balancing of the total demand for goods at the ruling price level and the ability of the economy to satisfy such demands when fully employed. In a closed economy a Keynesian budget would be in equilibrium when $D_p + D_g = Y_{fe}$, that is, when private demand and government demand equalled the full employment output with no tendency for prices to rise.

If $D_p + D_g > Y_{fe}$, there will be excess demand and inflation will ensue. If $D_p + D_g < Y_{fe}$, then there will be insufficient demand to buy all the output that could be produced and unemployment will result. Ideally, taxation is levied in such a way as to prevent depressions and inflation, and enable resources to be made available for government use.

In an *open* economy the stabilization measures are widened to achieve equilibrium in the balance of payments. When the balance of payments is in deficit there is an excess of imports over exports which results from domestic demand being greater than domestic supply. Imports are drawn in to fill all or part of the inflationary gap. If imports fill only part of the gap, then domestic prices will rise, exports will be harder to sell in foreign markets and imports will become more competitive in domestic markets. The trade deficit will get worse.

In recent years balance-of-payments considerations have been crucial determinants of government taxation policy. When international deficits occur taxes will be raised (a) to reduce the rate of rise of prices; (b) to reduce the demand for imports; and (c) to reduce the domestic demand for goods which may then be exported.

The relationship between revenue and expenditure

If taxation is no longer required to match expenditure dollar for dollar or pound for pound, what exactly is the relationship between revenue and expenditure? This may be illustrated by distinguishing between the long run and the short run.

Long run. If the government of a country is to provide for a large part of individuals' needs, then taxation will need to be set permanently at high levels. In other words, in the long run government revenue and expenditure are closely connected.

Short run. On the other hand, year-by-year changes in tax rates will not be determined by parallel changes in expenditure but by the needs of stabilization; the achievement of full employment without balance-of-payments difficulties or price inflation. Indeed, if unemployment rises, taxes are likely to be lowered and government expenditure raised. In times of inflation and balance-of-payments troubles, taxes may well be raised and government expenditure cut simultaneously. Thus in 1968 the British government not only increased taxes but cut back on projected expenditure as well. And in the United States, far from a tax increase going to balance increased government expenditure in a financial sense, Wilbur Mill's Ways and Means Committee only granted President Johnson his 10 per cent tax increase in 1968 on condition that government expenditure was cut as well. Conversely, in his budget of 1959 Macmillan's government in Britain cut a wide variety of taxes and increased government spending at the same time.

Summary on the aims of taxation

The function of the state may be summarized briefly. Politicians make value judgements (or interpret the value judgements of the majority) about what constitutes the proper distribution of income. They then try to produce that output of social goods and merit goods in the quantities and proportion that would be produced if that distribution of income were achieved, if there was perfect knowledge, if all externalities could be internalized and if there were no market imperfections.

Most descriptions of the aims of taxation start by saying that taxation is required to finance government spending. This is misleading. If that were all that was required of taxation, a benevolent government would abolish taxation and finance all its expenditure by printing money or borrowing it. Of course, this would be inflationary in all likely circumstances and of course the financing of government expenditures is an incidental role of taxation. The aim of taxation is to reduce private consumption and private investment so that the government can provide social goods and merit goods and subsidize the poor without causing inflation or balance-of-payments difficulties. And of course taxation must not be set so high as to reduce private activity to such an extent that unemployment results.

Changes in the tax rates therefore are not dictated simply by changes in government expenditure. They may just as well be brought about by changes in private consumption, changes in private investment or changes in the size of the national income which can be produced in conditions of full employment.

The basic function of taxation, then, is to reduce the demands made by the private sector on the country's productive capacity. And yet it is true that taxation has other objectives: income redistribution and growth in national income, for example. Is it not then oversimplifying to say that taxation is basically a deflationary device?

Taking the case of equity, with the two notable exceptions dealt with in chapter 6, governments do not normally tax the rich to make them poorer. What the authorities in effect do is to subsidize the poor and then look round for the most 'efficient' way of dealing with the inflationary pressure the subsidy implies. And 'efficient' taxation is levied in a way that aids redistribution (see chapter 9), helps stimulate growth (see chapter 10), and generally reinforces rather than conflicts with the various policy objectives in pursuit of which governments spend money.

2 Definition, Classification and Taxonomy of Taxes

Having described the circumstances which make taxes necessary, we describe in this chapter the vocabulary and basic tools of tax analysis.

Definition

Defining a tax is a matter, for economists, of describing the economic functions of taxes and making sure that everything that operates in this way is covered by the definition. The *Concise Oxford Dictionary* defines tax as 'contribution levied on persons, property or business for support of government'. But, as we have seen on page 23 the 'support' of governments able to print or borrow money may be a trivial function of taxation now that the principles of Keynesian public finance are understood. It is true that local governments may be dependent on local taxes for finance but central governments can and do print money and borrow to pay for some expenditures. They levy taxes, not to provide funds, but to control private expenditure, so that $D_p + D_g = Y_{fe}$. If we were to alter Fowler's definition to read 'contribution designed to reduce private expenditure', it would make more sense in economic terms. A meaningful and comprehensive definition of tax would be one which was stated in terms of income flows: 'a tax is any leakage from the circular flow of income into the public sector, excepting loan transactions and direct payments for publicly produced goods and services up to the cost of producing these goods and services.' In other words, loan repayments to government departments are not taxes and neither are the prices paid in Britain and the USA for postal services. But profits made by nationalized postal services are, for our purposes, taxes levied on postage.

Social security contributions are generally regarded as taxes although they might at first seem more analogous to prices paid to other nationalized industries. The reason for classifying such payments as taxes can be illustrated with reference to British National Health Insurance. This is a uniform levy on all employed males (different rates apply for females and self-employed persons). The insurance aspects of the scheme are illusory and it is much more realistic to regard this as a tax. National Health Insurance is not optional. Benefits are not related as with private schemes to one's past record of claims. The premiums do not cover the whole of the cost of claims and the government has an open-ended commitment to make good whatever shortfall arises. These contributions are raised when deflationary measures are required – like any other tax – not when the fund is low. And these contributions fit our definition of taxes.

A more problematical aspect of answering the question 'of what do taxes consist' is presented by what may be called *taxes in kind*. The usual method by which the authorities get the goods and services they require is to outbid the private sector in a free market and raise general taxation by whatever sum is necessary to deal with the inflationary effects of this expenditure. Another method, however, is for the government to use its judicial power to commandeer the resources at or below existing market prices. This will be less inflationary than buying in the market and so will necessitate a lesser increase in general taxation. The difference between the price to the government in a free market and the price paid under compulsion is a burden borne by the seller of the good or service in question and is analogous to a tax imposed on the sellers of such goods. A man whose house he values at £10,000 and which is required for motorway development by the government is in the same position if the government forces him to sell at £4000 as if the authority had offered him the £10,000 and then subjected him to a tax of £6000.

Compulsory purchase is an extremely common way of dealing with the inflationary impact of government expenditure and it is particularly important in times of war. It is then normal for governments to commandeer strategic materials, ban or ration what they regard as frivolous consumption, forbid or curtail private firms from raising prices and, most important, conscript labour. It is interesting to speculate on how much the United States would have to pay in soldier's wages in order to persuade half a million young Americans to go to Vietnam voluntarily. It seems by no means impossible that the abolition of the draft would necessitate an average rise in soldier's pay of $4000 per man if enough volunteers were to be found. In this case one could say that 1 per cent of the United States government expenditure is 'financed' by special taxes in kind levied on the army in Vietnam (Fisher, 1969; Altman and Fechter, 1967).

For purposes of exposition and for reasons of space we shall, however, do no more than acknowledge the existence of taxes in kind and concentrate in this volume on monetary taxes.

There is one other grey area in the definition of taxes. It is sometimes convenient to talk of subsidies as being negative taxes. Analytically this makes quite a lot of sense. For example, in Figure 2a a move of the income line from AB to CD can represent the effects of an income tax of AC, whereas a cash subsidy equal to CA would cause the reverse shift in the income line from CA to AB. Similarly in Figure 2b a tax of CB/OB on good x would cause a shift of the income line from AB to AC, while a governmental contribution towards the cost of buying good x of CB/OB would cause a shift in the income line from AC to AB.

There is one respect in which taxes and subsidies are not exact opposites. Taxation as a whole is designed, among other things, to reduce private expenditure in order to allow governments to spend without causing inflation. But subsidies are not designed to increase private expenditure in general. They are designed to increase the private expenditures of specific groups, of specific products, or in specific areas. Of course subsidies do, generally, have inflationary effects.

Subsidies are clearly being regarded as negative taxes by those who, like Brown and Dawson (1969), advocate negative income taxes. It is argued for a variety of administrative and efficiency reasons that the various subsidies should be consolidated into the income-tax structure. Instead of giving a subsidy to everyone who has children, for example, the income-

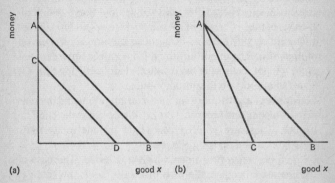

(a)   good x   (b)   good x

Figure 2

tax rates would be altered so that the rich paid a little less in tax and the poor get a negative income tax. If all redistributive payments were handled in this way they would be consolidated into one 'tax' with positive rates for high incomes and negative rates for low incomes.

In this volume we will deal mainly with positive taxes. For a more rigorous discussion of the distinction between taxes and subsidies, readers should consult Shoup (1969, pp. 145–8).

Taxonomy of taxes

The terminology of tax analysis can be discussed by distinguishing four features of taxes. The first two will provide a basis for the classification of taxes.

Classification

1. Each tax has a set of administrative arrangements for its collection. Income tax is paid *direct* by the taxpayer to the authorities, while sales taxes are paid by consumers of goods

and services but reach the government *indirectly* through the retailers who act as a collecting agency.

Taxes can therefore be classified as 'direct' or 'indirect' in accordance with the administrative arrangements for their collection. But important as these arrangements are for public administrators, Hicks (1946) has pointed out that a definition in terms of the tax base is of more interest to economists. Hicks prefers to classify taxes as being taxes on *income* or taxes on *consumption*. The important thing from an economist's point of view is not that a sales tax is collected indirectly but that it is levied in proportion to consumption.

However, a classification into consumption and income taxes is incomplete because there are direct taxes which fall on neither. These are *property* taxes and include estate duty, wealth taxes and real estate taxes.

2. Each tax has *a base* upon which it is levied. The base of income tax is income, the base of a sales tax is the value of sales, and the base of tobacco taxes is the weight of tobacco sold.

Table 2 classifies taxes according to the tax base and lists the major forms of taxation. Notice that the bottom line describes taxes as being *specific* or *ad valorem*. Specific taxes are those like the British tobacco tax at 504·375p per pound weight which is levied on the volume of the tax base. *Ad valorem* taxes are those like British long-term capital-gains tax which at 30 per cent is levied on the value of the tax base.

'*Progressive*', '*proportional*' and '*regressive*'

3. Taxes also have *a rate* or series of rates. The rate of corporation tax in Britain is $42\frac{1}{2}$ per cent, the rates of income tax range from zero to $88\frac{3}{4}$ per cent, and the rate of petroleum tax is 22p per gallon.

These rates may be *progressive*, *proportional* or *regressive*. These terms are often used loosely and require rigorous definition. A progressive tax is one which takes an increasing proportion of income as income rises, a proportional tax takes a constant proportion of income, and a regressive tax takes a declining proportion of income as income rises. As Table 3

Table 2
Taxation Classification

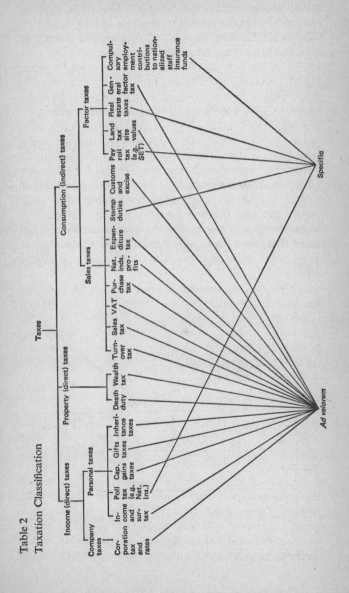

shows, progressive taxation does not simply mean that the rich pay more than the poor. This is true even in the case of the regressive tax. A progressive tax is one where the proportion of income going in tax rises with income.

Table 3
Tax Liability

Income	Regressive		Proportional		Progressive	
£10,000	£100	1%	£100	1%	£100	1%
£100,000	£200	0·2%	£1000	1%	£2000	2%
£1,000,000	£300	0·03%	£10,000	1%	£30,000	3%

Figure 3 shows the proportion of income taken in taxation under three different tax regimes. 1 shows a progressive tax, 2 shows a regressive tax, and 3 shows a proportional tax. The steeper the slope of the tax line, the more progressive the tax regime. The steeper the negative slope, the more regressive.

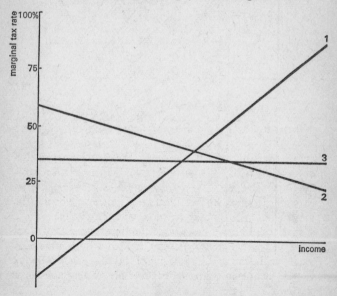

Figure 3

Bracewell-Milnes (1967) points out that measuring the progressiveness of a tax regime may not tell us very much. If you want to know how important the tax is in redistributing income from rich to poor, for example, the mere slope of the marginal rate of tax line will tell you little. Figure 4 shows two marginal tax lines. 1 is more progressive than 2, but 2 redistributes incomes to a greater extent.

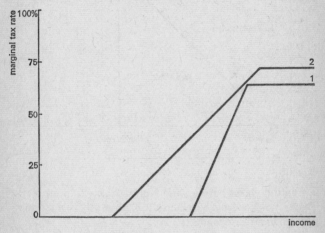

Figure 4

To get a meaningful picture of what a tax regime is like and how it affects the distribution of income, it is necessary to know not only the progressiveness – slope of the marginal tax line – but the 'height' – the maximum marginal rate of tax – the 'minimax point' – the minimum value of the tax base on which the top rate of tax is levied – and the starting point – the minimum value of the tax base upon which tax is levied.

Bracewell-Milnes's measure of the 'intensiveness' of taxes takes all these things into account. In Figure 5, AB is the marginal income-tax line. The height of this tax regime is 90 per cent at the minimax income EF, and the starting point is at income EA.

The intensiveness of the tax system is estimated as a ratio:

the area of intension over the minimax income (ABGE/EFBG) or the area of intension over the whole minimax area (ABGE/DCFE).

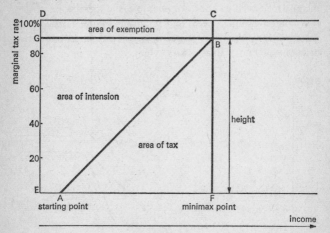

Figure 5

4. Fourthly, taxes have a variety of possible *effects*. Table 4 which is adapted from Seligman (1958), shows the relationship between these various effects.

The first important division of the effects of taxation describes the extent to which the person whose income, expenditure or property forms the tax base, bears the burden of taxation implied by pre-tax income, expenditure or property ownership. Suppose a man is earning £1000 per annum in an income-tax-free economy, for example, and the government decides to impose a proportional income tax of 10 per cent. What we are considering here is what happens to the £100 expected income-tax liability. *No escape* describes the extent to which the taxpayer fulfils the governments expectation and pays them the £100 and bears the burden of this tax. The consequences will be a fall in the consumers real income, necessitating a reduction in his savings, leisure or consumption of other goods.

On the other hand, the taxpayer may escape in whole or in part from this expected tax liability. This may lead to a loss of

Table 4

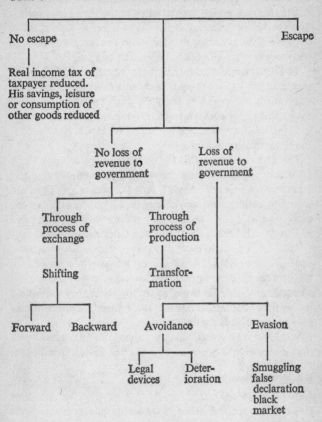

revenue to the government, the loss possibly occurring because of *evasion*. For example, the taxpayer may take such illegal action as making a false declaration to the effect that his income is less than £1000. Or legitimate steps may be taken to *avoid* taxes. Such a step – one which conforms to the letter of the law but not the spirit of the law – is available to our income-tax payer. He may be able to turn himself into a company whose income is £1000 per annum and sell his company for a capital sum. If capital is untaxed or taxed at a lower rate, the taxpayer can in this way get the present value of the future income tax-free. Or the tax base can *deteriorate*. This would happen in our example if the taxpayer decided to do less work and so earn less income as a result of the imposition of a tax.

To illustrate the effects when there is escape but the government still gets its money, we take the case of a payroll tax levied at so much per employee. If a firm, employing ten men, faces the imposition of a tax whose base is employees and whose rate is £5 per head, the expected impact of this is that it will reduce the companies profits by £50.

The firm can escape this tax by taking steps to improve its process of production in such a way as to raise pre-tax profit by £50 (or more or any part of it). Post-tax profits may be maintained by cutting down on other costs, by getting men to work more overtime, or by getting the ten employees to work more effectively. This reaction is called the *transformation of taxes*.

The firm could also escape by taking measures through the process of exchange. Faced with an increase in costs of £50, the firm may increase prices and *shift the tax forward* to consumers, cut the men's wages, or cut the prices they are willing to pay their suppliers of raw materials, thereby *shifting the tax backwards*. (This is the main subject of chapter 4.)

We now have the vocabulary to say a lot about taxes in a way that is economical of space. Consider the British income tax.

UK income tax

Administration: Direct
Base: Money income after allowances for family commitments
Rate: Progressive
Starting point about £600 for a married man with two children
Minimax Income about £20,000
Height 88¾ per cent.
Affects shifting: believed rare

Avoidance:
1. Deterioration popularly believed common, but conclusive evidence lacking.
2. Numerous legal escapes exist.

Evasion:
Common with spare-time work and with people who are paid in cash transactions. 3 per cent in the United States; no estimate for Britain.

International variation of revenue structure

In Britain and the United States a vast network of taxes exists. In the Bahamas almost the only source of revenue is import duties. In Monaco profits on state-run gambling is the principal form of taxation. Each country uses its own combination of the taxes available.

Table 5 shows the composition of the tax burden in five major countries. Interesting features of this table include the fact that income tax is a less important source of revenue in Britain than in the United States, that the United States is not bottom of the list with respect to social security contributions, and that company-profits taxes are most important to the revenue of the United States.

Table 5
Distribution of Tax Revenues 1965–6

	Taxes on households (mainly income tax)	Social security contributions	Other direct taxes (mainly company taxes)	Indirect taxes
Sweden	44·7	15·7	5·4	34·2
USA	34·1	16·8	16·4	32·7
GB	31·4	15·6	5·9	47·3
West Germany	23·3	28·9	6·9	41·0
France	11·9	37·0	5·2	45·9

3 Efficiency Criteria

We have described how the need for taxation arises and we have introduced the terminology of tax analysis. The rest of this volume will be devoted to considering how the authorities go about choosing the tax base. In this chapter, six criteria which may be used in choosing the tax base will be described. Students who would like to see how little thought has changed in this regard should consult Adam Smith (1776) and see how his 'canons of taxation' resemble what is to be said here. In Part Two of this volume we consider alternative approaches to the choice of an optimal tax regime.

Equity

It is clearly a desired characteristic of taxes that they be fair. Apart from the ethical desirability of equity, there is the practical need for taxes to be acceptable to the tax-paying public. If taxes are generally believed to be inequitable the consequences may range from widespread evasion to revolution.

Two classes of equity are distinguished. The first, *horizontal equity*, describes the equal treatment of equal people. This principle is unchallengeable as an ideal and is not impracticable of operation. People of equal incomes, for example, might be required to pay the same income taxes. All people who smoke twenty cigarettes per day would be required to pay the same in specific tobacco taxes. The second class is *vertical equity*, which describes the treatment of taxpayers who are unequal with the appropriate degree of inequality. While vertical equity also has great merit as an ideal, it is very hard to achieve in practice. This is because there are so many views held as to what *is* the appropriate degree of inequality. To some people the appropriate degree of inequality of income taxation will be served by a proportional tax, while others feel that progressive income taxes are more equitable.

The attempt to achieve vertical and horizontal equity together is never easy and can produce ludicrous results. In Britain, vertical equity is pursued by progressive income tax which is designed to make taxation vary appropriately with variations in income, and also through a policy of giving income-tax reliefs which vary with commitments, for example, family size. This is designed to give appropriately unequal treatment to people who have unequal commitments. In the interests of horizontal equity, all parents get an income-tax allowance of the same amount, i.e. £115 per head, irrespective of income. This leads to the anomalous situation in which a rich man, whose marginal rate of tax is $88\frac{3}{4}$ per cent receives a subsidy of £102·06, whereas a person too poor to pay tax at all, and presumably the one whom government subsidies are designed to help, gets no subsidy via the system of tax allowances.

The discussion of equity in taxation has produced two important and fundamentally opposed concepts of what is fair. The first, the subject of chapter 8, holds that equity is served by making the tax payment proportional to the degree of benefit derived from government expenditure. The second, which is dealt with in chapter 9, holds that vertical equity is attained when taxes are paid on the basis of ability to pay, those who can best afford it paying the most in taxation.

Neutrality

The second criterion by which taxes are judged is neutrality: the extent to which the tax avoids distorting the workings of the market mechanism. In Western economies the majority of decisions about what to buy, how much to save and so forth are made by a comparison of the benefits of these actions with the costs involved. Any taxation which is related to any economic activity will clearly distort this comparison of costs and benefits. An income tax reduces the benefits of work without making work less arduous. A tax on beer increases the cost without increasing beer's desirability. Thus taxes on motor vehicles not only remove cash from the private sector – which is the prime function of the tax – but in cases where demand is at all elastic distort consumers' choices between cars and other goods. Such a tax might encourage some people to buy a helicopter and reduce expenditure on cars and many other goods, and encourage others to buy a motor bicycle and increase their purchases of other goods. Such a tax would not only raise revenue but cause consumers to reorganize their consumption patterns so that these no longer reflected the balance between the benefits of consumption and the costs of production. The private sector would not only have less money to spend; it would be encouraged by the tax to spend sub-optimally what it had left.

On neutrality grounds, a general sales tax is preferable to a specific tax on one good only. At least with a general sales tax all goods are made dearer so there is no reason for irrational reallocation of purchases. Similarly, taxes on goods which are subject to inelastic demand cause less distortion than taxes on goods subject to elastic demand.

The distortion of choices which is involved in the process of taxation is known as the *excess burden of taxation*. The goal of neutrality is the minimization of this excess burden. This is dealt with at greater length in chapter 7.

Too much should not be made of neutrality, however. In the case of demerit goods such as cigarettes and alcohol, taxes may be chosen precisely because of their non-neutrality.[1] Moreover, a government which is short of strategic materials may tax the use of these materials specifically to reduce private consumption below the level which the free market would dictate. Similarly, taxes may be imposed on crowded roads deliberately to drive some consumers on to their second choice of travel route.

Certainty

The third criterion employed in assessing the worth of various taxes is the certainty with which the authorities can look for-

1. It is true that taxation of cigarettes and tobacco may be so common and so heavy because, showing inelastic demand, they are good revenue raisers. The demerit argument may just be a high-sounding excuse.

ward to the revenue which should accrue. Tax revenues almost never turn out exactly as expected. This has serious implications for the success of the taxes in (a) bringing about the required delicate balance between aggregate demand and full employment output in the economy, and (b) fulfilling the various microeconomic objectives of taxation, such as horizontal equity, which were envisaged when the tax strategy was initiated.

There are four main aspects of certainty.

1. The *certainty of incidence*, which is the subject of chapter 4, concerns the certainty with which the authorities can predict the effective incidence of taxes. Say the government wishes to pursue an active fiscal policy to improve health by reducing cigarette smoking; its ability so to do will be constrained by the certainty with which the effective incidence of various taxes is known. An effective discriminatory tax on tobacco requires knowledge of the extent to which such a tax is shifted backward to the tobacco sellers' profits or forward to the employers of tobacco smokers in the form of higher wages.

2. The *certainty of liability*, concerns the ease and certainty with which liability to tax can be assessed. A completely general retail sales tax scores well here but taxes like the British *selective* employment tax leave a great area of doubt about whether tax has to be paid or not. Wealth taxes where tax officials have to value the taxpayer's property leave a great deal to the discretion of the tax official. A common example of such uncertainty is in the assessment of how much of a car used for business and pleasure to allow as a business expense. This has two disadvantages: (a) the taxpayer is left in doubt about his liability, and (b) there is great scope for bribery of tax officials.

3. The *evasion ratio* measures the certainty with which the authorities can extract the revenue from those liable to tax, i.e. the extent of evasion. Income tax is not a very good tax on this score because people often decline to disclose the full extent of their incomes. On the other hand, there is virtually no evasion of tobacco duty. According to Rey (1965) the Italian General Sales Tax has an evasion ratio of at least one-third.

Fiscal marksmanship deals with the certainty with which the authorities can predict the revenue that will fall due to be paid in the year in question. This will depend on their ability to forecast the values of the macro- and microeconomic variables upon which tax revenues depend. That is to say, the certainty of the revenue from income tax depends on the Treasury's ability to forecast income. The certainty of the tax revenues from motor duties depends upon the ability to forecast car ownership. Allan (1965) has shown that in the U K between 1951–63 the certainty with which revenues were predicted varied widely. Table 6 shows that the fiscal markmanship of oil, tobacco and alcohol duties was very much better than that of profits tax and protective duties.

Table 6

Miscalculations of Revenue by Taxes, U K, 1951–63 inclusive; Error Percentage of Estimated Revenue

Oil duties	1·9
Tobacco duties	1·9
Income tax	2·3
Alcohol duties	2·9
Surtax	4·1
Profits tax	5·9
Purchase tax	6·4
Protective duties	11·8
Stamp duty	13·8

Source: Allan (1965).

Evidence

The fourth criterion is the evidence of taxes. This is the extent to which the taxpayer is made aware of his tax payments. Because of the long-run relationship between government expenditure described on page 22, taxation is in fact the price the public pays for the goods and services provided by the government. In the democratic process, it is one of the functions of taxation to help consumers to decide how much of social and merit goods and redistribution they truly want by giving information about their cost. The more evident taxation is, the better equipped people are to vote for their first choice of public-sector size.

Thus income tax, which is taken from individuals directly, is very evident but payroll taxes, which may be passed on or may be absorbed by producers, are very nebulous in their effects. They help finance the public sector without giving the public much evidence about the cost.

The evidence of a tax may not be regarded as a merit. A benevolent and wise paternalist may find taxes which have little evidence are the best way to get people to agree to what is good for them. In times of war when massive sums have to be raised it may be best for morale to concentrate on taxes which are not evident.

Administrative efficiency

Another criterion is administrative efficiency, which relates to the percentage of revenue dissipated in collection expenses. As Table 6 shows, this is seldom a very high percentage. But it is important to note that it is not only the authorities who bear expenses. When one adds the cost to taxpayers of their own time and that of expensive tax lawyers and accountants the cost–revenue ratio may become considerable. And indeed, when we come to consider Kaldor's criterion in chapter 6, we shall see, as Merrett (1965) shows in terms of the British capital-gains tax, that the inflationary effects of administrative costs may well be greater than the total deflationary effects of the tax.

Table 7
Administrative Costs: Percentage of Revenue, UK, 1965–6

SET	0·1
Customs & Excise	0·86
Estate duty	0·93
Income & supertax	1·40
Stamp duty	2·03

Net expenditure restraining effect

Kaldor (1956) has asserted that, as the principal aim of taxation was to restrain private expenditure, its success in so doing should be a criterion by which taxes are judged. Because different taxpayers have different marginal propensities to consume, the amount of private expenditure restrained will be different, depending upon whom these taxes fall. Thus a tax which falls on people with an average marginal propensity to consume 0·75 has a net *expenditure restraining effect* of 75 cents for each dollar of tax-revenue. Kaldor called the net expenditure restraining effect the 'economic efficiency' of taxation. This seems a little extravagant – our other criteria also measure levels of economic efficiency – nevertheless we shall use Kaldor's terminology.

Economic efficiency is discussed at greater length in chapter 6. There, on page 70, Table 10 gives some recent estimates of the economic efficiency of various taxes. It shows that from the lower rates of income taxes £100 of revenue allows the government of a fully employed country to buy £100 worth of goods without causing inflation. But £100 worth of revenue raised from company taxes will only enable the government to buy £50 worth of goods, while £100 raised from capital taxes allows the government only to buy £10 worth of goods without causing inflation. (We have assumed for the moment that the multiplier effects which attach to both the taxation and the expenditure are the same.)

Partial equilibrium analysis

For the most part, each of the above efficiency criteria will be investigated in a partial-equilibrium framework. Shoup (1969) has cast serious doubts on the efficacy of this technique for analysing the effects of most tax changes. Partial analysis of the kind used in chapter 4 – where the elementary theory of the firm is used to analyse the effects of profits taxes on prices – will not tell us anything, according to Shoup. This is because we have ignored the effects on the firm's costs of production when (a) its suppliers react to the profits tax, and (b) the government spends its enhanced revenue. Partial-equilibrium analysis is only useful when three conditions are met: the tax must not effect costs of other products; the tax must not alter the demand for other products; and the money must be spent by the government in such a way as to leave unaltered the cost and revenue schedules of the firm. The ideal tax for partial-equilibrium analysis is narrowly based, small in amount, and is spent on, say, overseas aid.

The problem of the effects of government expenditure on the cost structure can be dealt with by assuming that government expenditure is given. This is not an unreasonable assumption to make because in the case of the British government at least expenditure plans are drawn up first and changes in tax rates are made with this given rate of expenditure in mind. It is then possible to compare the consequences of raising revenue by an increase in income tax with the consequences of increasing, say, a general sales tax.

Even when Shoup's three conditions are not met we may learn something from a partial approach. For example, in the case of profits tax and the firm, if we can establish that firm's profits tax by raising prices by the full amount of the tax, we have a basis – by no means flawless – for guessing that the firm's suppliers of raw materials and components react in the same way. If we know what proportion profit is of price, we can make predictions about the effects of changes in profits tax on the price level.

Nevertheless there is no doubt that the real world is general and that analysis which is to be of predictive value should be as general as possible. If the world is too complicated or if our tools of analysis were too primitive we shall not scorn the partial approach. We shall remember that a general equilibrium is the sum of many partial equilibria, and if we understand some of the partial equilibria we will be that far on the way to understanding the whole.

We will, however, recognize two warnings. Firstly, partial conclusions are to be treated with caution. Taxes may perform very well as measured against one efficiency criterion but may be most undesirable because of an extreme offence against another criterion. Secondly, in order to make decisions in political economy it is necessary to set up a system of trade-offs between the various efficiency criteria. At the moment the information necessary to make such rigorous judgements implied by the term trade-off is unfortunately not available. Strong ordering is perhaps all that is possible. And in chapter 11 we set up the basis for reducing the virtues and vices of various taxes to a common denominator. However, when one remembers that this system involves value judgements about weighting and that empirical evidence is either lacking or uncertain, it is clear that economists who venture to offer suggestions for fiscal policy should do so with humility, if at all.

4 The Incidence of Taxation

The concept of incidence

Let us define the 'burden of taxation' as the decline in real income that is suffered as a result of the tax. Here we are considering the effects of the tax alone and ignoring the benefits that flow from government spending of the revenue.

Fiscal analysis is considerably complicated by the fact that the burden of taxation may not be borne by the individual or firm making formal payment. For example, to use Hicks's (1946) terminology: the *formal incidence* of British purchase tax is upon wholesalers whereas the *effective incidence* is (mainly at least) on the consumers who pay higher retail prices. The wholesalers shift the tax burden forward to the retailers who shift it further forward to the consumers. This is called *forward shifting* of taxes. If the wholesalers reacted to the imposition of purchase taxes by negotiating lower prices for the goods they buy from the manufacturers this would be *backward shifting* and some of the effective incidence of taxation would then be on the manufacturers. Some or all of the tax burden may remain with the wholesaler and to that extent the effective and formal incidence of the tax are the same.

When a tax is imposed there are seven ways in which the burden can be disposed of:

1. The formal taxpayer may bear it all.
2. The formal taxpayer may shift it all forward.
3. The formal taxpayer may shift it all backward.
4. The formal taxpayer may shift some of the burden forward and the rest backward.
5. The formal taxpayer may shift some of the burden forward some backward and bear the rest himself.

6. The formal taxpayer may bear some of the burden and pass the rest forward.

7. The formal taxpayer may bear some of the tax and shift the rest backward.

It is therefore apparent that the formal and effective incidence of taxes may be very different. And it is clearly very important for the purposes of fiscal analysis and the formation of tax policies to know, not only who hands the cash over to the government (the formal incidence), but also to have an accurate picture of who bears the burden of such taxes (the effective incidence). We shall start by considering some *a priori* evidence.

The incidence of business taxes

Lump-sum taxes

We start by considering lump-sum taxes on business. These are taxes which do not vary with output or profit such as local rates or licence fees. We assume that businessmen maximize profits.

Taking first the case of the firm in perfect competition. Figure 6 shows a firm in equilibrium selling output OQ_0 at price OP_0.

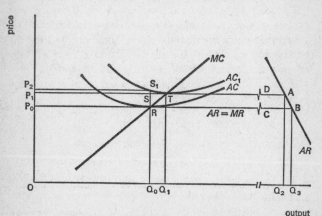

Figure 6

This equilibrium is determined by the intersection of the marginal cost and marginal revenue schedules at R when average cost (AC), which includes normal profits, is just covered. The imposition of a lump-sum tax on this firm raises the average cost curve to AC_1. But this tax is not shifted forward to the consumer. Neither the marginal cost curve nor the marginal revenue curve have been affected so that the firm is still in equilibrium at R, maximizing profits (in this case minimizing losses). In the short run the firm bears all the lump-sum tax and makes a loss $P_0 P_2 SR$.

In the long run the supply curve of the industry rises from CB to DA and price rises from OP_0 to OP_1. The output of the firm is increased from OQ_0 to OQ_1 and the output of the industry is reduced from OQ_3 to OQ_2 by the elimination of some firms. It is not possible to say which firms will be eliminated.

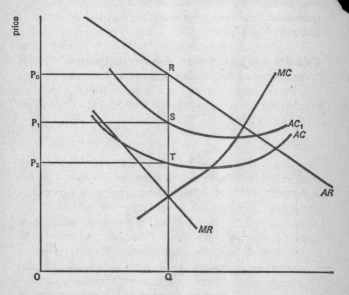

Figure 7

without more information. If there are inter-firm differences, the least efficient will be eliminated. If all are identical, all will be eliminated together and will be replaced by a smaller number of new firms.

And secondly, the firm with monopoly power. Lump-sum taxes on profit-maximizers facing downward sloping demand curves are not shifted forward in the short run or the long run. Again this is because neither of the important marginal schedules is affected by such taxes. The firm whose cost and demand conditions are described in Figure 7 is in equilibrium at R selling output OQ at price OP_0, making monopoly profits P_2P_0RT. When a lump-sum tax is imposed on this firm the average cost rises from AC to AC_1. But as neither marginal schedule is affected the firm is still in equilibrium at R. Price remains the same and the firm bears all the tax. This reduces the firms profits to P_0RSP_1, the tax being equal to P_1P_2TS; the difference between the pre-tax and post-tax average cost ST times the output P_2T.

We have, then, what may seem at first sight to be a somewhat unlikely result. Setting aside the case of the long run in perfect competition on the grounds that perfect competition is only a limiting case and does not describe any real economy, profit maximizing firms do not alter their prices or output in response to lump-sum taxes.

Profits taxes

The same will be true of flat-rate profits taxes like the British corporation tax of $42\frac{1}{2}$ per cent. *In perfect competition* price is given in the short run and no increase in prices, to pay taxes, is possible. In the long run some or all firms will find that normal profits, as reduced by taxation, are no longer sufficient to make it worthwhile to continue and they will go out of business. Prices will then rise so that after-tax profits are equal to former normal profits. In the long run, as with the lump-sum tax, the effective incidence will be on consumers. *The case of a monopolist* paying a 50 per cent corporation tax is represented in Figure 8. The line UV, which is halfway between the average cost and average revenue schedules, represents the $AC + 50$ per cent profits-tax line.

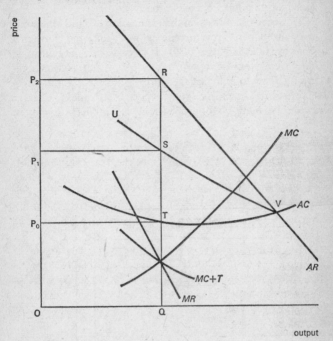

Figure 8

The firm is in pre-tax equilibrium selling OQ units at price OP_2 and making maximum profits P_2RTP_0. The tax liability on these profits is P_0P_1ST, or 50 per cent. After-tax profits are P_2RSP_1. After-tax profits are halved but no change in pricing or output policy is required. This is because neither of the determinants of the profit maximizing price and output policy (marginal cost and marginal revenue) is affected by profits taxes.

The effective incidence of profits taxes is the same as the apparent incidence if firms maximize profits. Profit maximizers do not pass on profits taxes. If the firm is already maximizing, a change can only be for the worse. In other words to maximize 50 per cent of profits requires the same price and output policy as maximizing 100 per cent of profits.

This conclusion rests on the assumption of short-run profit maximization. However, empirical work since the pioneering done by Hall and Hitch (1939) has suggested that most firms do not act in a way which approximates to short-run profit maximization. They usually set their prices in some variant of the 'cost plus' system. For example price is set equal to average cost plus a mark-up for profit. In this case profits taxes may be passed on.

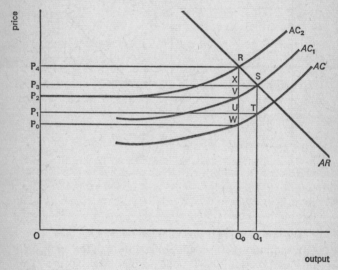

Figure 9

In Figure 9, AC is the average cost curve of *a firm which follows a full-cost pricing policy*. AC_1 is AC plus the mark-up the firm thinks reasonable, and AC_2 is AC_1 plus a 50 per cent profit tax, so that $RV = VW$. The firm is in pre-tax equilibrium selling OQ_1 at price OP_3. It makes profits of P_3P_1TS.

After the imposition of a 50 per cent profits tax, the firm

moves to a new equilibrium selling OQ_0 at the higher price OP_4 in order to preserve its reasonable profits mark-up. Pre-tax profits are now P_0P_4RW, of which taxation takes half, i.e. P_2VWP_0. The question is: who pays this tax? Is the effective incidence of this profits tax on the companies, on the customers, or is it shared?

The consumers are clearly paying some of the tax as they are now paying a price which is higher by P_3P_4. They buy output P_4R, so in effect they pay P_4RXP_3 of the tax.

The company's tax share can be ascertained in numerous ways. The simplest is to observe that the company is making the same profit per article, i.e. $ST = RV$, but is selling a smaller output P_1U as opposed to the former output of P_1T. So the firm's profit is reduced by $UTSX$.

The effective incidence of this tax, then, is shared by the firm paying $UTSX$ and the consumers paying P_4RXP_3. It should be noted also that an additional loss of welfare is suffered by those consumers who now find the goods too dear as a result of tax increases. This extra loss of consumers' surplus is represented by the area RSX.

This result depends on the assumption that firms are rational in their treatment of taxes; that the desired mark-up for 'profit' refers to profit after tax. Unfortunately, there is some evidence that large numbers of firms do not take profits taxation into account in determining investment and pricing policies. They set their profit margin and then regard taxation as a nasty surprise. In so far as firms do ignore profits tax, changes in such taxes will not be passed on to consumers.

Sales tax

Taking the case of a specific tax – TV in Figure 10 – the imposition of a sales tax will cause a shift in the marginal cost and of the average cost schedules upwards by the amount of the tax, TV. This leads to a new equilibrium with a higher price, OP_3, and a lower output OQ_0.

Revenue receipts are P_1P_0YX: the amount of the tax times the output. Taxpayers pay higher prices equal to P_3P_2ZR. The company pays $P_1P_0YX - P_3P_2ZR$ (the total tax bill minus the

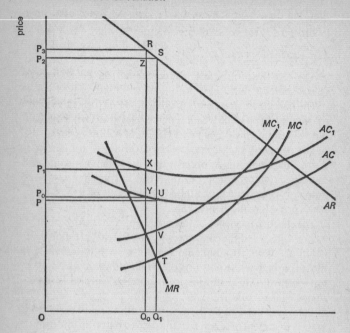

Figure 10

consumer's share). Some of the tax has been shifted forward to the consumers. But the company also suffers an increase in average cost from P to P_0 and profit is further eroded by a reduction in sales from Q_1 to Q_0. Profit is reduced from P_2SUP to $P_1 P_3$RX. Also, consumers who now find the good they wanted to buy too dear suffer a loss of consumer surplus represented by the area RZS.

In the case of a firm which operates on the basis of a fixed mark-up on average costs, the incidence can be traced as in Figure 9. Again a specific tax (RV) is partially shifted forward from producers to consumers.

To sum up the argument so far, 'profit maximizers' will pass on sales taxes and taxes which otherwise effect marginal costs, but will absorb profits taxes and taxes on overheads, while 'full-cost' firms will shift all kinds of taxes.

The extent of business-tax shifting

Having established on *a priori* grounds when business taxes will be shifted, we now consider what determines the *extent* to which shifting takes place. We shall see that various results will follow from taxes imposed on different industries depending on the elasticities of the various cost and revenue schedules.

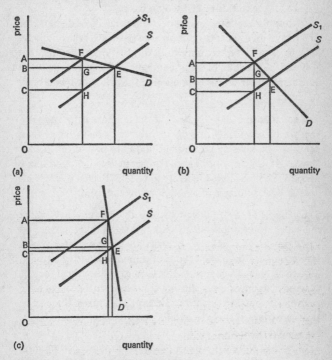

Figure 11 The elasticity of demand

Figure 11 shows the incidence of a tax on a commodity. S is the pre-tax supply curve. S_1 is the post-tax supply. D is the demand curve. The figure shows the effective incidence of the tax under varying demand-elasticity conditions, while supply has the same elasticity in each of the three cases, (a), (b) and (c).

The tax raised in each case is equal to AFHC. BCHG is borne by the firm and ABGF is shifted to the consumer. (There is an excess burden FHE; p. 82.)

It can be seen that the greater the elasticity of demand, the less the firms will shift the tax on to consumers. Figure 11 (a) shows elastic demand and very little tax shifting. Figure 11 (c) shows very inelastic demand and a great deal of tax shifting. Figure 11 (b) shows the intermediate case.

Two considerations which affect the elasticity of demand for products with respect to price and are especially relevant to tax shifting should be mentioned. Both arise from the fact that demand is a function of the price and availability of substitutes. The demand for beer is a function of the price and availability of lager.

1. The breadth of the tax base. If the tax base is narrow, e.g. the tax increase only applies to beer but not to lager, then sales will be severely curtailed if taxes are passed on to consumers. If, on the other hand, the tax is broadly based like a general sales tax, sales are likely to be less affected by price increases and shifting is more likely to take place.

2. Openness of the economy. If the economy in which the tax increase is to be applied is open, in the sense that there are no great physical or political barriers to the entry of untaxed foreign goods, then the elasticity of demand for such goods will tend to be high. The opposite will tend to be the case if there is a closed economy. So tax shifting is less likely in the case of state sales taxes than in the case of Federal sales taxes. State sales taxes are more likely to be avoidable by crossing a state boundary to do one's shopping.

Figure 12 shows the incidence of a tax on a commodity. Again S is the pre-tax supply curve, S_1 represents post-tax supply and D is the demand curve. This time we hold demand steady in (a), (b) and (c), and examine the effective incidence of the tax with various elasticities of supply.

The tax raised in each case is ACHF; BCHG is borne by the

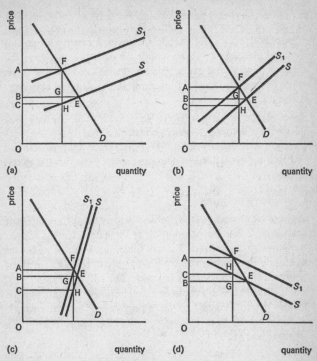

Figure 12 The elasticity of supply

firms concerned, and ABGF is passed on to the consumer. (Again there is an excess burden FHE.)

It can be seen that the greater the elasticity of supply the more tax shifting takes place. (a) shows elastic supply and a great deal of tax shifting (ABGF is very large); (c) shows inelastic supply and very little tax shifting (price has only risen by BA); and (b) is an intermediate case.

Figure 12 (d) shows the special case of a negative elasticity of supply; the downward sloping supply curve. In this case the tax shifting is more than 100 per cent. The pre-tax price is OB. After a tax of AC, price rises to OA, a rise of BA which is greater than the total tax payment.

When supply has a negative slope, the smaller the elasticity the greater the price rise resulting from sales tax increases.

Supply elasticity, then, tends to increase forward shifting and demand elasticity tends to reduce forward shifting. And the relative buyers' and sellers' shares of the tax burden can be estimated as the ratio of the supply to the demand elasticity. Thus

$$\frac{\text{Elasticity of supply}}{\text{Elasticity of demand}} = \frac{\text{buyers' share}}{\text{sellers' share}}.$$

So that if the elasticity of supply is 2 and the elasticity of demand is 1, the buyers will bear twice as much of the burden as the sellers.

Capitalization of taxes

An important aspect of the problem of identifying the bearers of the ultimate burden of taxation is the extent to which such burdens are capitalized. Table 8 illustrates the case of a firm operating in a market where (line 1) it can sell £40 worth of goods of which real-estate tax takes £10 and other costs £10, leaving the firm with a profit of £20. The market value of such a firm is determined at five years purchase of after-tax profit, giving a return to new investors of 20 per cent. The firm is worth (line 1) £100.

Table 8

Real estate tax	Other costs	Output	Profit	Value of firm at five years purchase
10	10	40	20	100
0	10	40	30	150
20	10	40	10	50

Lines 2 and 3 show the effects on the value of the firm of the abolition and doubling respectively of the real-estate tax – assuming other costs and sales remain constant and that no shifting takes place. It can be seen that the effective incidence of these tax changes is on the capital value of the firm. The return on that capital value remains unaltered at 20 per cent. There is in fact no annual burden of this tax, just a once-for-all burden borne in the year of the tax change.

This can best be illustrated by considering the position the new owners of this firm if the firm is sold. If capitalization takes place as shown in Table 8, they will get 20 per cent return on their capital irrespective of the existing tax rate. The burden to such new owners is the same whether the tax is £0, £10 or £20 per annum.

The model used to illustrate capitalization is unlikely to approximate to any real world market, and capitalization is unlikely to be as extensive or as simple as here explained. However, there is no doubt that tax changes do affect capital values, and to the extent that this capitalization does take place we have another problem to solve in identifying the ultimate burden of taxation.

The general nature of the problem

So far we have taken a partial equilibrium approach and apart from the last section where supply and demand elasticities were taken together from the others, examined each of the things which affect tax shifting in isolation. This has let us see just what the effects were taken together from the others. This has let us see just what the effects of each on its own is. But in order to predict what will happen in the real world we need (a) a great deal of accurate information and (b) a general equilibrium approach.

Table 9 is a first step towards a general equilibrium approach. Here are listed those factors which increase the likelihood or extent of shifting on the left and those which inhibit tax shifting on the right. No rigorous system of trade-offs is attempted. All we can say is that the more entries there are on the left the more extensive tax shifting is likely to be.

Caution

This has been no more than an introduction to the problem of incidence, showing what kind of *a priori* reasoning has been brought to bear on the problem. Its main function is to show

Table 9

Shifting	No shifting
Full cost pricing (all taxes)	Profit maximization (profit taxes and taxes on business overheads)
Inelastic demand	Elastic demand
1. broad tax base	1. narrow tax base
2. closed economy	2. open economy
Elastic supply	Inelastic supply
Decreasing costs	Increasing costs

that effective incidence need not be the same as apparent incidence and that the obvious need not happen.

This sort of *a priori* analysis can aid understanding of the problems but it is to empirical studies that we must look for hard evidence of where the effective incidence of taxes lie. Unfortunately, conclusive empirical work is in short supply.

The British SET (the tax on employment in service industries), imposed in 1966, led to steep rises in the prices of some services and to no rise in the prices of others. Some firms paid all the SET and other firms made their customers pay it all. Others again used the consumers' expectation of SET-inspired price increases to increase prices by much more than costs had risen. In 1967 when British gasoline taxes were increased by 1·67p, the producers' recommended prices rose by 1·67p per gallon. But there followed intensification of the prices war between retailers and soon afterwards the biggest companies reduced their recommended prices by 1·25p. It seemed that the producers were paying 1·25p of the 1·67p tax. The retailers who cut prices also paid some. And while some consumers had part of the tax increase shifted forward onto them, others were actually paying less for their petrol. But was this really a consequence of the tax increase? Would the price war have hotted up anyway? Would the oil companies have reduced recommended prices anyway? It seems likely that the tax rise brought forward changes which were already under consideration. In that case how much of these changes do we attribute to the tax increases?

This all illustrates the problems involved in quantifying the extent of tax shifting.

We have introduced the notion of shifting with reference to company taxes and consumption taxes. But what of personal income taxes? It appears, at first sight at least, to follow from the marginal productivity theory of wages that income taxes are not shifted backwards to the companies in the form of successful demands for higher wages and salaries. One's tax payments do not effect one's productivity in any obvious way; so how can they affect wages?

There are several possibilities for shifting.

1. The increased tax may lead to a reduction in the supply of labour and so to a rise in marginal revenue productivity (MRP) and so to a rise in wage rates. (The likelihood of this is discussed more fully in chapter 5.)

2. The labour market may not be in equilibrium; MRP may be higher than pre-tax wage rates and labour may be able to negotiate compensating wage increases passing some or all taxes on to company profits.

3. The company may not be maximizing profits and may readily agree to compensating wage increases which it will then shift again – on to the consumers.

Despite the lack of hard evidence it seems likely that some shifting of income taxes takes place. It seems improbable, for example, that the pre-tax salaries of some company chairmen would be so high were it not for the fact that they pay such high income taxes. Some of their tax burdens are very probably passed on to shareholders and consumers.

Finally, what of the shifting of the taxation of real incomes which operates through the taxation of goods and services? The prominence of cost-of-living considerations in collective bargaining suggests that a significant proportion of wage rises are invoked by price increases. Taxes give rise to price increases and so presumably to increases in wage rates. It is likely that consumers shift some of the tax burden back on to the companies who probably pass some or all of it back again in higher prices. The wage–price spiral is at least partly a tax-shifting phenomenon.

One looks hopefully to the econometricians for clear evidence on the effective incidence of taxation. Unfortunately there are too few observations of tax changes, and too many difficulties concerning the unravelling of cause and effect to make measurement easy. To take the most obvious difficulty – we want to measure the effect of profits tax on pre-tax profit. But taxes are usually raised in cyclical upswings (when profits are rising anyway) and lowered in depression periods (when profits are falling). Further this is a broad-based tax and Shoup (1969, ch. 1) argues that it is not permissible to ignore problems of what the government does with the money. This has not stopped attempts to study incidence using econometric methods. The studies of Krzyaniak and Musgrave (1963), Laumas (1966), Roskamp (1965) and the Canadian Royal Commission (1966) have suggested that extensive shifting of corporation taxes is usual in the USA, India, West Germany and Canada respectively. Whereas Cragg, Harberger and Meiszkowski (1967) and Gordon (1967) have found support for the zero shifting hypothesis.

It looks a bit like a draw; and even though the models which show that no shifting takes place are the least unrealistic I am not willing to declare anything more decisive than a draw. I will stick to my intuitive guess that shifting to consumers of profit taxes is usual. If investors are doing anything rational they are buying a stream of future income after tax. To some extent, then, one would expect their reactions to change in after-tax profits to raise pre-tax profits. It is hard to accept the logic of the zero shifting hypothesis, i.e. that it will make no difference to price in two years' time whether profits taxation has been halved or doubled.

5 Taxation and Incentives

One of the great unsettled questions which require firm answers before optimal tax policies can be designed is the problem of how much taxes affect the supply of labour, of savings, of investment, and of the willingness to undertake risky investments which promise high if uncertain rewards. We need to know to what extent taxation, by lowering the rewards of economic activity, alters its supply.

Income tax and the supply of effort

We shall concentrate in this chapter upon the effects of income taxes on the supply of labour for three reasons: because most work has been done on this aspect of the problem; because all taxes fall ultimately on someone's income either by reducing its quantity or (in the case of non-income taxes) reducing its real value by raising prices; and because the principles involved are the same for the choice between income and leisure as for the choice between consumption and saving.

Two questions have to be answered. Firstly, how does the level of taxation affect willingness to work? Does high taxation give less incentive and so produce less work? Secondly, how does the way in which a given level of income tax is levied affect effort. Does progressive taxation weaken incentives more than proportional taxation?

The theory

Figure 17 in chapter 7 (case 2) shows how an income tax comes between a taxpayer and his allocation of time between work and leisure. We want to see if he can be expected to do more or less work.

Figure 13 shows two effects of a tax which lowers the income line from AB to AC. The income effect is the move from R to

S and that from S to T is the substitution effect (the extent to which substitution of leisure for work is induced by the reduction in the rewards of effort or reduction in the price of leisure). But notice that the income effect tends to increase work and the substitution effect tends to reduce it. If the income effect is strongest, the result of the tax will be an increase in the supply of effort, as in (b), where the individual will work harder to pay his taxes and maintain spending power. If the substitution effect is stronger, as in (a), the supply of effort will decline – people work less because the rewards are lower.

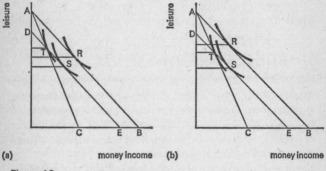

(a) money income (b) money income

Figure 13

We cannot say on *a priori* grounds whether raising taxes will increase or decrease work effort.

On the other hand, it can be shown that proportional taxes are preferable to progressive taxes on incentive grounds. A change from a proportional tax to a progressive tax which would leave the taxpayer paying the same tax on the basis of unchanged income will lead to a decrease in the supply of effort. This is shown in Figure 14 (a) and (b), where AC is a proportional income tax but DE is a progressive tax. The change to a progressive tax causes a reduction in work effort, and a deterioration of the tax base in both cases.

Notice that in (b) more effort is supplied with a progressive tax than with no tax, but that less work is done than with a proportional tax in both (a) and (b).

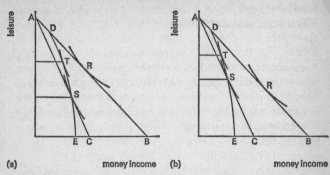

(a)　　　　　　　money income　(b)　　　　　　　money income

Figure 14

A proportional tax is shown to be less bad or more good for incentives than a progressive tax in its effect on this individual.

Empirical evidence

There are a number of difficulties common to all empirical studies of this problem. For example, there is a shortage of observations, as well as the difficulty that one cannot observe the difference between a world in which there are taxes and one in which there are none.

Most of the studies have been of the survey type where people are asked to state how taxes affect them. This is a most unsatisfactory way of finding out about the effects of taxation for a number of reasons. These include the likelihood that answers will reflect taxpayers' dislike of taxes rather than how they in fact react to them and the fact that consumers themselves may not know how they react.

Brown and Dawson (1969) have surveyed the evidence and find that a concensus from these researches suggests, firstly, that tax is a disincentive for 5–15 per cent of the population. Disincentives are greatest among those without families, the middle-aged, the rich and those not living in large cities. Secondly, a somewhat smaller proportion react to taxes by working harder. The highest proportion of these is found among the young, those with large families, those who live in large cities and have little wealth. A large proportion of people

...dom to vary their hours of work and so are not ... one way or the other.

Income taxes and supply of savings

If we accept that people have a marginal propensity to consume of between 0 and 1, then raising taxes will at best leave savings unaltered and at worst reduce savings out of a given income by the amount of the tax. In fact we can with some confidence say that an increase in taxation will lead to a reduction in savings and vice versa.

Now it is possible to show that, as in case 3 in chapter 7, page 86, an individual who has his tax payments changed from paying income tax to paying the same amount in consumption taxes will increase his savings. The trouble is that in practice such a tax change would not, for most people, mean paying the same in taxes. Some would pay more in taxes and others would pay less. Some would increase savings and others reduce them. We cannot say on this basis what would happen in aggregate.

We know of course that the rich save more than the poor and that while income taxes are usually progressive, consumption taxes are normally regressive. For this reason a tax regime which concentrates on taxing consumption will produce a higher level of savings. Kaldor's (1956) progressive expenditure tax was designed to overcome the egalitarian bias in favour of income taxes. Kaldor favoured his expenditure tax because by raising the price of consumption, savings would be encouraged. We must remember, however, that such encouragement would be irrational except in circumstances in which expenditure tax was thought likely to fall in the future. There is no good saying we won't buy now because the prices are too high, if the items are going to be as dear or dearer in the future.

Taxation and the distribution of risk

As well as having effects on the supply of effort and the supply of saving, taxation may have important effects on the pattern of investment. 'Taxes which reduce the rewards of successful investment may be a disincentive to risk-taking and this could have adverse effects on economic growth.' The more people are encouraged to put their money into savings accounts or in boxes under the bed, the less entrepreneurship there is.

In Figure 15(a), OA is the pre-tax opportunity line, showing a saver's possible combination of yield and risk. The higher the risk the greater the yield. OB shows the opportunity line after a proportional income or profit tax. We cannot say *a priori* whether the reduction in yields brought about by the tax will lead to an increase or a decrease in the riskiness of the investments undertaken. As with our model of the supply-of-effort problem, it will depend on the shape of the indifference map. If it is as in IC_2^a, risktaking will increase. But if it is as in IC_2^b, the riskiness of investments undertaken will fall.

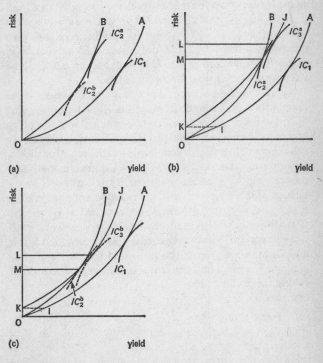

(a)

(b)

(c)

Figure 15

Again, all we can say is that this consumer will take more risk if this proportional tax is replaced by one that does not vary with profits and which raises the same revenue. This is illustrated in Figure 15 (b) and (c), where OJ is the opportunity under a lump-sum tax of KI. In both cases the consumer will move to higher indifference curves (IC_3^a and IC_3^b) and take the higher risk OL compared with OM.

But this apparent conclusion, that the more progressive a tax is with respect to the tax base the stronger will disincentives be, only applies to the individual. The tax changes will only be of the kind depicted here for those whose incomes and opportunities are the same as those depicted in Figures 14 and 15. For everyone else the change will mean either an increase or a decrease in the taxation on the basis of their existing tax base. And as we saw in Figure 15 (a), we cannot say whether the movement will be of the type to IC_2^a (where risk was increased) or of the type to IC_2^b (where risk was decreased). And as we saw in Figure 13, we cannot be sure if the substitution effect will be stronger or weaker than the income effect.

Apart from the *a priori* evidence that progressiveness in the taxation of a given amount from each individual is an inhibiting factor, and a suspicion based on the empirical work that high taxation is on balance slightly inhibiting, there is not much one can say about the effect of taxation on incentives and on the distribution of investment. More emphatic conclusions await econometric work which unfortunately is frustrated by the lack of usable observations – tax rates do not change often enough and when they do so much else changes too. However, it seems likely that incentive effects of highly progressive taxes are more important than the evidence is able to show, and Brown and Dawson are prepared to guess that the supply of effort could be increased by 1 per cent if certain steps were taken to reform the tax structure.

Part Two

In Part One we dealt with some preliminary problems of taxation, introduced some of the terminology used in discussing taxes, and described some of the features of taxes which are generally thought desirable. In Part Two we go deeper and investigate the various fundamental approaches to taxation. We try to answer the question: What is it that tax legislators are (or should be) trying to maximize, minimize or optimize in designing a tax regime?

6 The Revenue Minimization Approach

The point is made and emphasized from time to time in this volume that the principal objective of taxation is to regulate private expenditure on goods and services to whatever level will produce full but not over-full employment. This suggests the first of the approaches to taxation, i.e. that the relative efficiencies of taxes be judged by their abilities to restrain private expenditure. If the authorities employ those taxes which are most effective at controlling private spending they will minimize the amount of revenue necessary for control.

Much of the popular discussion of fiscal alternatives is conducted as though each tax had the same ability, pound for pound, to fulfil this basic function. That was all right in pre-Keynesian times. When the government was simply trying to raise enough revenue to cover its own expenditures it was quite sensible, for example, to choose between taxes on the rich and taxes on the poor on the basis of which tax imposed the least sacrifice on individuals pound for pound. But now that taxation is not expected to balance expenditure but to control private expenditure to a required level such pound for pound comparisons make little sense. It may be that the tax which imposes the least sacrifice also produces the least reduction in private spending.

Kaldor (1956) has called the effectiveness of a tax in reducing private spending its *net expenditure restraining effect* or its *economic efficiency* (E_T), which can be defined as

$$\frac{\text{Change in private expenditure,}[1] \triangle C}{\text{Change in revenue, } \triangle R};$$

1. C is used here to denote all private spending – both for consumption and investment.

$$E_T = \frac{\triangle C}{\triangle R}.$$

Thus a tax change which increased revenue by £100m and induced a fall in private expenditure of £80m would have an economic efficiency of $80/100 = 0.8$.

The importance from the point of view of Keynesian public finance of the economic efficiency of taxation can hardly be stressed too strongly. If it is required to reduce private expenditure by £100m, then the government will have to choose a tax or taxes whose net expenditure restraining effects are £100m. A greater expenditure restraining effect will produce unemployment and a smaller expenditure restraining effect will allow excessive expenditure and inflation. In order to choose a combination of taxes which reduces private expenditure by just £100m it is necessary to have either accurate estimates of the economic efficiencies of various taxes or extraordinary luck.

It will be seen that the economic efficiency of taxes (being the extent to which a change in such taxes alters private expenditure) is ascertained from the marginal propensity to consume of the relevant taxpayers. Just as different taxpayers have different marginal propensities to spend, so will economic efficiency vary from tax to tax.

As was indicated in chapter 4, it is difficult enough to find out who the real taxpayer is let alone to find out his marginal propensity to use scarce resources. However, some of the esti-

Table 10
The Economic Efficiencies of British Taxes

Tax	Economic efficiency
Income taxes (reduced rates)	1·0
Income taxes standard and surtax rates	0·67
Taxes on expenditure	0·8
Taxes on dividends and trading incomes	0·5
Taxes on capital	0·1

Source: Dow (1964), p. 198, note (f).

mates which have been made are given in Table 10. The figures refer to the British economy, and are compiled from data of the period 1945–60. Although no great claims as to their accuracy (at the time when they were compiled, let alone for all time) were made, they will be accepted without further question for the purpose of exposition in this chapter.

Several important consequences follow from the existence and importance of the phenomenon of economic efficiency of taxation:

1. Two equi-revenue taxes will not necessarily have the same stabilizing value. £100 raised by increasing the reduced rates of income tax will reduce private expenditure by £100. But a £100 increase in taxes on profits will only reduce private expenditure by £50.

2. In a fully employed economy any addition to the government's programme of expenditure on investments or consumption or real goods (as distinct from transfers), will have to be matched, not by an equal increase of revenue as in popular debate, but by a larger increase in revenue. The exception to this rule is when the increased revenue comes from the lower rates of income tax. In a fully employed economy any net increase in government spending must be met by a cut in real private spending. So if the government wishes to increase its expenditure on real goods to the value of £100, then it must depress private expenditure by an equal amount or cause inflation. This £100 reduction in private expenditure can be effected either by increasing the lower rates of income tax and taking in £100 extra revenue, or by increasing the standard and surtax rates to bring in £144 extra revenue, or by increasing profits taxes to raise an extra £200 of revenue, or, finally, by raising capital taxes sufficiently to bring in an extra £1000 in revenue.

3. This requirement that the reduction in private expenditure should match the increase in public expenditure pound for pound, applies when the government buys real goods or makes real investments. But how much will private spending need to be reduced in order to counter the inflationary effects of

transfer payments such as sickness benefit, old age pensions and investment grants? This will clearly depend upon the *net-expenditure-producing* effect of the transfers (E_G), defined as

$$\frac{\text{Change in private expenditure, } \triangle C}{\text{Change in government transfers, } \triangle G},$$

$$E_G = \frac{\triangle C}{\triangle G},$$

so that the amount of extra revenue required to balance a transfer is

$$\triangle R = \triangle G \frac{E_G}{E_T},$$

in other words, the change in government transfers multiplied by the economic efficiency of these transfers divided by the economic efficiency of the chosen tax.

Different kinds of transfers will have different economic efficiencies; national assistance and other payments to the very poor are likely all to be spent and to have economic efficiencies of $1 \cdot 0$. Investment grants, on the other hand, may have most of their effective incidence on company profits, in which case an economic efficiency of the same as profits tax seems a reasonable assumption, i.e. $0 \cdot 5$.

Using these guesses at the expenditure-creating effects of government transfers, Dow's estimates of the economic efficiency of taxes, and the equation just mentioned, it is possible to work out how much of each tax would be required to balance each type of transfer.

Example 1. It is proposed to increase investment grants at a cost to the exchequer of £100. The required reduction in private spending is to be brought about by increasing taxes on personal expenditure. How much will the revenue required be?

$$£100 \times \frac{50}{100} \times \frac{1}{0 \cdot 8} = £62 \cdot 50.$$

Government transfers of £100 will have to be balanced by £62·50 of increases in taxes on private expenditure.

Example 2. It is proposed to increase old-age pensions at a cost to the exchequer of £100m. The required reduction in private expenditure is to be produced by taxing company profits. What will be the required additional yield of profits taxes?

$$£100m \times \frac{100}{100} \times \frac{1}{0·5} = £200m.$$

Government transfers of £100m will have to be met by an increase in tax revenues of £200m.

Thus far we have said nothing about the multiplier effects associated with this government revenue and expenditure process, though these are clearly important. The reduction in private expenditure brought about by taxation will have a negative multiplier effect on income, while the increased resource use brought about by government expenditures or transfers will have positive multiplier effects on income. This does not affect the foregoing analysis, however, because we have assumed implicitly that changes in resource use brought about by government revenue and expenditures are subject to equal multipliers.

This assumption, although it may be a reasonable approximation, is unlikely to have universal validity. Expenditure cuts brought about as a result of increased income taxes are likely to be the subject of different multipliers to those spending increases which result from government expenditure on civil engineering projects, for example. This is so because income will be subjected to a different level of savings at each round of the multiplier, depending on the propensities of various people involved. Different government expenditures involve different people, which involve different levels of the marginal propensity to save.

Thus allowing for different multipliers (k) being appropriate to different kinds of revenues and expenditures, the change in revenue required to meet a given government expenditure in a fully employed economy is

$$\triangle R.E_T k_T = \triangle G.E_G k_G,$$

$$\triangle R = \triangle G \frac{E_G k_G}{E_T k_T}.$$

If taxes are primarily designed to reduce private expenditure, would it not be a good idea to choose between taxes on the basis of which taxes were most efficient at reducing private expenditure? Kaldor, who developed the concept of economic efficiency, appeared to think so when he commended his 'expenditure tax' on the grounds that it would have a higher economic efficiency than the income taxes which it would replace. This approach to choosing the tax base could be called the revenue-minimization approach. It would involve reducing those taxes where a large part of the impact is on savings and which do not reduce spending by very much, such as death duties, super-tax and taxes on company profits. The reduced rates of income tax and sales taxes and other taxes on consumption would be increased. If this policy were adopted the government could produce the desired reduction in consumption with a much smaller total revenue. A higher proportion of incomes would be left in private hands. At first sight at least taxpayers could be expected to welcome such a change in policy.

It must be said right away that the gains that would accrue to taxpayers as a result of increased use of taxes with high economic efficiencies would be somewhat illusory. Certainly, taxpayers as a whole would have higher after-tax incomes. But this would only be made possible because a larger volume of savings out of post-tax incomes occurred under a revenue-minimizing regime. As soon as people tried to spend these savings, and in so far as they did spend such savings, the tax rates would have to be raised. So that while taxpayers as a whole would get to keep a larger fraction of their incomes, they wouldn't get to spend this money.

The illusory nature of the gains, however, does not invalidate the case for revenue-minimization. Firstly, it does not matter very much to the individual that his joy may be in some sense irrational. As long as he feels better, he is better. And secondly, the gains are only illusory for taxpayers as a whole. If there is a general rise in spending because people have been allowed to keep more of their incomes, then tax rates will have to rise. So *everyone* can't consume more. But the *individual* can do so, knowing that the little extra he consumes is not going to increase his own tax burden by a noticeable amount. It is therefore possible for the individual to derive real benefit from the extra saving that would be made possible by a revenue minimizing regime, in the knowledge that, if he ever fell on hard times, he could always use these savings.

A general word of caution

It must be noted that the approach suggested by the works of Keynes (1936, 1940) and Kaldor (1956) to the problem of how much tax to raise and which taxes to use, is based on a view of the expenditure–income relationship which is still controversial (see Ackley, 1961, ch. 10). It is assumed that, having identified the need for deflation, the government, in order to introduce the right degree of deflation, must know the average marginal propensity to spend of the payers of various taxes and must so weight the taxes according to the MPC of the taxpayers that precisely that amount of tax-increase will be ascertained which will produce the required reduction in private resource use. This assumes that there is a simple functional relationship between consumption and income of the kind depicted in Figure 32 (p. 159), namely, that consumption is a decreasing function of income.

But other more realistic theories of the income–consumption relationship have been advanced. Duesenberry (1949) believes the long-run relationship to be one of proportionality. As income grows the proportion saved remains constant. But income does not grow smoothly and it is well known that the proportion of income saved does vary over time. Duesenberry explains these variations in terms of a lag in the reaction of consumption to fluctuations in income. Thus when income falls consumers are most reluctant to alter their established consumption patterns and reduce savings wherever possible. When income starts to rise again the level of savings is restored before consumption resumes its increase. So that with cyclical fluctuations in income growth there are short-run variations around a basically proportional relationship between consumption and income.

Another family of interpretations of the relationship between consumption and income is the normal or permanent-income hypotheses which make consumption a function, not of income alone, but of some wider index of ability to pay, taking into account such things as expected future income, and current assets as well as current income. These make consumption much less flexible with respect to income changes. While the Keynes and Kaldor model would expect an immediate response in consumption to changes in taxes, the permanent-income hypothesis suggests that, faced with a tax change, the burden may at first be placed on savings without much effect on consumption. Only gradually will the effect of taxes come to be felt on consumption. If the permanent-income hypothesis is better at explaining the reaction of consumers to taxpaying than the linear consumption function approach, then compensating tax policy becomes more difficult. Compensatory action may be taken but it may take a long time before consumption is affected. It is important to remember that the economic efficiency of taxes does not mean much unless a time period is specified.

British experience in 1966, 1967 and 1968 may support the permanent-income hypothesis. Successive deflationary measures failed to cut private expenditure. Some people kept up their expenditure by reducing their savings or incurred debts against expected future income rather than cut their consumption. Certainly cuts in consumption have been less than expected. But this may be explained by a series of once-and-for-all shifts in the consumption function. This is quite plausible because with prices rising quite quickly and rumours of devaluation and then the fact of devaluation, faith in the value of savings does appear to have declined slightly. Then again, failure to restrain the private sector may be explained by the faster-than-anticipated growth in money incomes. This fact combined with a slight fall in savings could be explained by shifts in the consumption function.

My suspicion is that permanent income best describes how the middle- and upper-income groups react to tax changes, with the very richest not showing any reaction at all. But linear consumption–income relationship clearly must hold for those who have no savings or only savings of a contractual nature. These people have little option but to cut consumption immediately or at most they can afford to let consumption lag only a short way behind income.

This suggests a tax strategem. The long-run fiscal objective of balancing the availability of resources in the economy with private- and public-sector demand should be undertaken, with a knowledge of the long-run relationship between consumption and income. This would entail the taxation of rich and poor in accordance with the various social and economic objectives discussed in this book. But in the case of compensatory fiscal policy (tax changes to deal with, for example, cyclical changes in demand), the burden of tax changes to suppress excess consumption or eliminate unemployment would be placed as firmly as possible on the lower-income groups. While we reject revenue-minimization as a general principle, it may be worth considering a revenue-minimization approach to the problems of short-run demand management.

As we can see from Table 10, a revenue minimization regime would imply concentration on taxes which bore heavily on the poor. It is well known that the marginal propensity to consume of the poor is highest. This may conflict with the distributional aims of government in two ways.

Firstly, as we observed in chapter 1, the government raises taxes in such a way as to reinforce (or to conflict as little as possible with) objectives pursued through its expenditure policies. One of the main items of government expenditure is support of the poor. It would be nonsense to pay for this by a revenue minimization approach which would concentrate taxation on the poor.

Secondly, a revenue minimization approach may produce undesirable distributional side-effects through its effects on the size of the national debt. A revenue minimization approach would imply a government deficit each year and a growth in the national debt. This implies a growing share of the national income going to national-debt holders, a progressive redistribution of income in favour of owners of capital. Meade (1964) has pointed out that this leads to a reduction in socialistic distribution which may be against the policy of the government and may also have undesirable incentive effects. As more and more of income is allocated to debt holders, more and more people have less and less incentive to productive effort.

Indeed, a person who wanted to produce a progressive shift in the distribution of after-tax income from the ownership of debt to productive investment and work effort, might advocate a revenue maximization approach. This would involve concentration on low efficiency taxes – supertax, taxes on capital, and so on – in order to produce budget surpluses with which to pay off the national debt. This would reduce the need for taxes to service the debt and gradually shift the distribution of the national income away from debt holders.

Another line of argument which can be used to support revenue maximization is that suggested by Duesenberry's (1949) work on utility. Thus it may be argued that the very fact of taxing the rich may confer benefits on the poor because it will reduce income differentials. Because of emulation, poverty is not only an absolute but also a relative concept.

Summary

Knowledge of the economic efficiencies of taxes is vital to successful macroeconomic control; but to choose taxes just because they had the highest economic efficiency (so as to minimize the total tax revenue requirement) would make no sense. There are many objectives to be pursued by taxation, not the least of which is income redistribution and this is inconsistent with revenue-minimization. To accept the principle that the government should raise all its revenue from taxes which have high economic efficiencies, involves the same sort of nonsense as suggesting that government expenditures should all have low economic efficiencies; for example, that the authorities should stop subsidizing the poor who spend it all and start subsidizing the rich who keep a lot of their marginal incomes.

At the same time, a recognition of the fact that different amounts of different taxes will be required to achieve a given reduction in private consumption is vital to successful macro-economic control.

As we shall see in later chapters, the economic efficiency of taxes is important in assessing the welfare effects of various taxes. The case against consumption taxes on the grounds that the choice between consumption and saving is distorted, is much weakened by recognition that saving and taxation are to a very large extent alternatives. When politicians make their value judgements as to what is a fair balance between taxation of the rich and taxation of the poor, or their guess as to which degree of progression in income tax causes least aggregate sacrifice, they should temper their judgement with the knowledge that the more the rich are taxed the greater will have to be the total money value of the tax burden.

7 The Neutrality Approach

Despite the problems of identifying the ultimate bearer of tax burdens, it is safe to say that all taxes fall ultimately on someone's income. Taxes either reduce income directly or reduce the real value of income by raising the prices of the things which income can be used to buy. It can be argued that a single tax on income would be the best tax because other taxes, while ultimately falling on income, so interrupt the flow of information in the market as to cause unnecessary inefficiencies.

The market economy works through the comparison by individuals of the benefits they will get from various activities with the costs involved. The market economy, steered by price-signals, produces the goods and services in the proportions which the individuals in the economy are willing to pay for them. It takes more effort to produce a car than it does to produce a bicycle – this fact is indicated in the relative prices of these commodities. And whether consumers purchase cars or bicycles depends on the amounts of money they are able and willing to pay. A rise in, say, the price of cars implies, therefore, that more people than previously are willing to pay the money that will induce workers to produce more cars. Profits in car-making will rise and more cars will be produced.

Such a market is in equilibrium where the consumers' marginal rate of substitution between goods is equal to the marginal rate of transformation between these goods.

When taxation enters the market it distorts the relationship between the costs of various actions and the rewards of such actions. It is sometimes said that taxation drives a wedge between the costs of production – marginal rate of transformation – and the benefits of consumption – marginal rate of substitution. This wedge is likely to mean a sub-optimal use of the country's resources: a use of the country's resources which does not reflect consumers' and producers' preferences.

Suppose that a tax is levied on cars while bicycles are left tax-free. This will lead to a rise in the price of cars and a reduction in car sales, and perhaps to an increase in the sales of bicycles. This change in consumption is not caused by any change in the relative real costs of production of these goods. The individuals in the economy have not only paid taxes but have suffered the excess burden of having their choices distorted by taxation. In the same sort of way the choice between income and leisure is distorted by earned-income taxes which lower the rewards of work. And taxes on investment-income distort the choice between saving and consumption by lowering the rewards of savings below what would be their value in an unfettered market.

The neutrality approach to taxation seeks a tax base which minimizes the excess burden of taxation, i.e. which minimizes the extent to which taxation distorts individual choices.

The Marshallian excess-burden proposition

Perhaps the simplest demonstration of the excess burden imposed on the economy by way of distorted allocation of the national income is provided by a Marshallian cardinal utility approach.

In Figure 16 (a) we graph the market for a commodity. In the absence of taxation, the market will be in equilibrium at E with output OG selling at OB per unit. If a specific tax equal to FD is imposed on this good, the supply curve will rise to $S + T$ and the market will be in post-tax equilibrium at F, with a smaller output OH and a higher price per unit, OA.

The revenue raised by this tax is equal to CD (the number of units sold) times DF (the tax rate), and is represented by area AFDC. Consumers have suffered a loss of consumers' surplus represented by area ABEF as a result of the imposition of the tax, and producers have suffered a loss of producers' surplus equal to area BCDE. But the loss of surpluses (ABEF + BCDE) is greater than tax revenue (ACDF) by FED. Thus

FED is an excess burden. Not only do taxpayers pay the government taxes (ACDF), but they suffer an excess burden FED, through the distortion of their choice between the commodity in question and the other goods available.

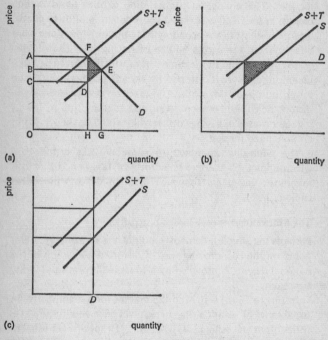

(a)

(b)

(c)

Figure 16

The existence of an excess burden demonstrable in this way is clearly dependent upon the extent to which choices can in fact be distorted by taxes. Hicks (1947) has shown that the excess burden varies with the elasticity of demand for the product in question. In Figure 16 (b) we have perfectly elastic demand and a large excess burden. In Figure 16 (c) we have zero elastic demand and no burden, while in (a) we have an intermediate case and an excess burden somewhere between the extremes. In (a) a large burden exists because the tax greatly distorts the consumers' consumption of the goods in question. In (c) no excess burden exists because the tax does not distort the consumption of the good in question at all. In fact, the taxation of a good which does not show any demand elasticity (and so no excess burden) will be the same in effect as an income tax raising the same amount of revenue but without reference to expenditure patterns. In both cases the consumption of other goods by taxpayers will have to be cut, and in neither case will the consumption of the good in Figure 16 (c) be effected. Nor will there be an excess burden associated with distortions of choices for this good.

The Marshallian excess-burden arises from the taxation of specific goods which distorts choices between the taxed goods and other goods. This burden might be avoided in three ways: firstly, by taxing goods which show no elasticity of demand; secondly, by taxing all goods equally (*ad valorem*) or, thirdly, by taxing income.

The Hicks–Joseph excess burden

The 'superior' neutrality of income taxes as compared with taxes on specific goods was demonstrated by Hicks (1939) and by Joseph (1939), using the techniques of ordinal welfare economics. The ordinal approach is an improvement on the cardinal because it allows us to compare the effects of different taxes on a consumer's welfare. The Hicks–Joseph proposition may be stated thus: taxes on income are preferred to taxes on specified goods because they do not distort the consumer's choices between goods.

In Figure 17 we consider the effects of income taxes or excise taxes on an individual. The aim is to show how a given tax payment can be made so as to reduce the consumer's welfare by as little as possible. The best tax regime will be the one which leaves the individual on the highest indifference curve. This model assumes perfect competition, a fixed supply of savings, a fixed supply of effort, and that the government requires a given revenue yield from this taxpayer.

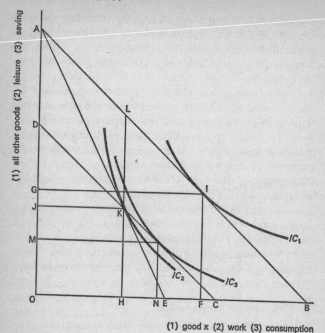

(1) all other goods (2) leisure (3) saving

(1) good x (2) work (3) consumption

Figure 17

Case 1. Figure 17 shows a consumer's indifference map of the choice between good x and all other goods (or money income). The consumer has a pre-tax income which will buy him OA of all other goods or OB of good x, or any combination of good x and other goods within the triangle OAB. The consumer will be in pre-tax equilibrium on his pre-tax income line AB maximizing his welfare on IC_1, consuming OF of good x, and spending the rest of his income OG on all other goods.

Let us assume that the government imposes a tax on good x. This will raise the price of good x from OA/OB to OA/OE, and the consumers after-excise-tax income line will be AE. The consumer can now choose between an unchanged quantity of other goods OA (and pay no tax), and OE of other goods, paying EB in taxes, or any combination on income line AE.

Faced with this new income line, the consumer will move from IC_1, which is now unattainable, to IC_2, which is the highest indifference curve attainable under this tax regime. The consumer chooses OH of good x, OJ of other goods, and pays KL in taxes.

Now let us consider the position of the consumer if the same amount of tax (KL) is raised by means of an income tax. The consumer's income line after an income tax of KL is represented by DC. The tax liability under an income tax is the same irrespective of how income is spent on combinations of x and other goods which are undisturbed by an income tax.

But DC passes through IC_2, at K, so it must be possible for the consumer to attain a higher level of welfare on the higher indifference curve IC_3. There he consumes ON of good x and only OM of other goods. So the consumer prefers paying income tax to paying the same amount in excise duty.

The income tax is preferred to the excise tax because it does not cause a reorganization of consumer's choices which is not dictated by changes in the costs of production. The excise tax has substitution effects sometimes called *announcement effects*. When the tax is announced the consumer is prejudiced against the good which is taxed. The neutrality approach can be restated as the search for a tax regime which minimizes substitution effects, i.e. the search for a tax base which will not shrink on the announcement of the tax.

Thus in Figure 17, the income tax was shown superior to the excise tax because while we were dealing with a given income, OA, the consumption of good x could be altered in response to tax changes.

Case 2. It is widely held that income taxes are not in fact the neutral taxes which we appear to have shown them to be in case 1. Does not the existence of income taxes have *disincentive effects*? Do they not distort the choice between income and leisure? Is the substitution effect of a tax which varies directly with income not a reduction in work?

Dropping the assumption of fixed supply of effort, Figure 17 can be used to illustrate the substitution effects of a proportional income tax and the excess burdens imposed by such an income tax as compared with a poll tax – a tax on individuals which does not vary with income.

In this case (case 2) the indifference map shows the consumer's choice of work (money income) or leisure. The pre-tax opportunity line is AB, showing that the consumer can have OA of leisure or OB of money income (work), or any combination of the two on AB. The consumer is in pre-tax equilibrium at IC_1, spending OF of his time working and spending the rest of his time OG in leisure.

AE is the opportunity line under a proportional income tax. As the amount of work increases so does the individual's tax liability. The taxpayer's choice ranges from taking all his income as leisure and making no money income and so paying no taxes, to working all of the time for a money income OB, EB of which has to be surrendered in taxes. The taxpayer is in equilibrium in this regime on IC_2. He chooses OJ of leisure and spends the rest of the time JA working. This leaves him a money income of OH after paying income tax of KL.

But revenue equal to KL could have been raised from this consumer by a poll tax of KL. The opportunity line under this regime is DC. It can be seen that the taxpayer in Figure 17 will reorganize his time under this poll-tax regime in such a way that while making the same poll-tax payment, AD = LK, he can achieve a higher level of satisfaction on IC_3.

Thus far we have shown that, *when required to pay a given amount in taxes*, the consumer will prefer to pay by income tax than by taxes on any of the goods he buys. Moreover, he will prefer a poll tax to any other form of income tax which distorts the choice between leisure and work.

Case 3. It is possible further to demonstrate the superior neutrality of a poll tax. Using Figure 17 we can drop the assumption of fixed supply savings and consider the choice between saving on the vertical axis and consumption on the horizontal axis. AB is again the pre-tax income; OF is consumed and OG is saved. If the government raises revenue by a tax on consumption the consumer moves to a new equilibrium on IC_2. If the same amount of revenue is raised by a tax on income or by a poll tax, the consumer can attain a higher indifference curve IC_3. So the Hicks–Joseph proposition argues from the point of view of the individual, that the poll tax or income tax is preferred.

The Morag reversal of the poll tax neutrality conclusion

Morag (1959) has pointed out that the Hicks–Joseph conclusion rests on the assumption of required yield. In all three cases (Figure 17), the government is attempting to raise a given revenue equal to AD. But in post-Keynesian times governments are not interested in raising a fixed sum of revenue. What is required of taxation is that it brings about a required amount of absorption of private expenditure. Taking case 3 opposite and dropping the assumption of required yield, it can be shown that a given reduction in private consumption can be brought about by raising less revenue under a consumption tax, and that consumers in fact 'prefer' taxes on consumption to poll taxes (or other taxes on income). The poll tax conclusion is reversed if we drop the assumption of required yield.

The Hicks–Joseph demonstration appeared to show that poll taxes and other income taxes would be preferred by consumers to taxes on consumption because the taxation of consumption distorted the consumers' choice between consumption and saving. In Figure 18, the consumer's pre-tax equilibrium is at A on IC_1. Out of a total income OH, he consumes OD and saves the rest DH. If the government raises revenue by a tax on consumption, the consumer moves to a new equilibrium on IC_2. If the same amount of revenue is raised by a tax on income or a poll tax, the consumer can attain a higher indifference curve, IC_3. So the Hicks–Joseph proposition argues, from the point of view of the individual, that the poll tax or income tax is preferred.

This conclusion, however, is reversed if we compare consumption taxes with poll taxes or with income taxes not on an equi-revenue yield basis but on the basis of each tax producing the same reduction in the individual's consumption. Notice that under the equi-revenue taxes, represented by price lines

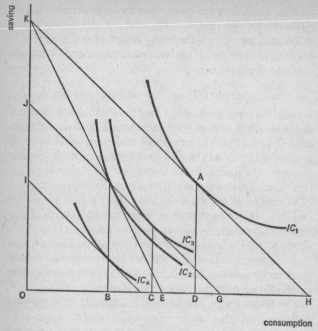

Figure 18

KE (consumption tax) and JG (income tax or poll tax), the reduction in consumption is not the same in each case. Under the 'inferior' (on an equi-revenue basis) consumption tax, the individual's consumption is reduced by DB, whereas the income tax or poll tax, while it is preferred on an equi-revenue basis, only reduces the individual's consumption by CD. If the same amount of restraint on consumption, BD, was to be achieved by an income tax, then the revenue required would have to be much higher, at KI, and the consumer would find himself in equilibrium on the much lower indifference curve IC_4. Thus the conclusion in favour of income taxes and poll taxes as against taxes on consumption is reversed when we recognize that the government is not trying to achieve a given revenue but is trying to induce a given cut in private expenditure.

Because, and only because, the consumer is willing to save more under a regime of taxes on consumption, can the government achieve the required reduction in consumption with a smaller yield with taxes on consumption. If consumers decide under this regime to save less, the taxation will have to be increased (or government expenditure cut) to stabilize demand. But illusory though these gains may be, the consumers demonstrably prefer revenue-minimization (see chapter 6) as an approach to getting each to cut his expenditure by a given amount. IC_3 is much higher than IC_4.

Friedman's general equilibrium model

The most obvious criticism of the Hicks–Joseph demonstration is the extremely partial nature of the model (see Figure 17). The assumption of perfect competition is a very restrictive one, and Friedman's general equilibrium model (1952) allows us to consider the situation in which goods are produced under conditions of increasing costs. Friedman's model also renders unnecessary the pre-Keynesian assumption of required yield.

In Figure 19, good x is produced under conditions of increasing cost *vis-à-vis* other goods. AB is the transformation curve of other goods into good x, showing that as the output of x increases the amount of other goods which has to be forgone increases as less and less suitable resources are switched to production of x. The curve CD is the transformation curve showing the production possibilities left open to private consumers after the government has decided how much of the national income it is going to pre-empt for the public sector. The public sector is going to pre-empt resources which could be used to produce DB of good x or CA of other goods. So that if inflation is to be avoided, the private sector must be taxed in such a way that it does not try to buy more resources than can be accommodated within the area OCD. Any point nearer to O than CD will imply unemployed resources, so that clearly the government's tax strategy is to raise whatever revenue is necessary to force the private sector to make a choice of good *x* or other goods which lies on CD. *Notice that the assumption of required yield is redundant. As long as private consumption is reduced to a point on CD the amount of revenue raised is irrelevant.*

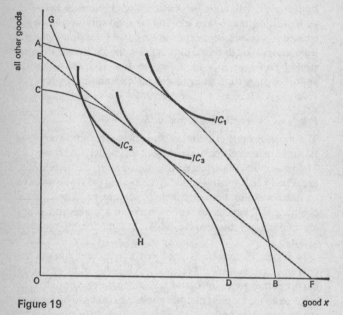

Figure 19   good *x*

If we assume an economy of identical consumers, Figure 19 can represent the case of the individual. Under an income tax, the consumer will be in equilibrium on IC_3. He will be faced with market prices which tell him about the rate of exchange at which he can swop good *x* for good *y*. This will be an optimal solution because the price will equal the rate at which they can be substituted one for the other in production (the marginal rate of transformation) and also equal to the rate at which the consumer is willing to swop *x* for other goods (the marginal rate of substitution between the goods).

But if the consumer is forced down on to CD by means of a

selective excise on good x, the position will no longer be optimal. Here the market price of good x is raised to a rate represented by GH. In this case the consumer will be in equilibrium on IC_2, equating his marginal rate of substitution for good x and other goods with the rate at which they can be substituted in the market, i.e. with their prices. But the price of x relative to other goods has been distorted and price does not reflect the marginal rate of transformation of good x into other goods that is possible in production. Taxation has driven a wedge between the marginal rate of substitution and the marginal rate of transformation, and the situation is non-optimal.

IC_3 is preferred to IC_2, so that a selective excise is shown to impose an excess burden upon the consumer by distorting his choice between good x and other goods.

It has been shown that taxes can cause burdens in excess of the financial burdens involved in having to pay them by getting between producers and consumers and by distorting price information inducing them to make irrational choices. So long as the tax base is flexible with regard to price, excess burdens will arise and the greater the flexibility the greater the excess burden. It has been shown that poll taxes have superior neutrality and the conclusion in favour of head taxes was based on the non-flexibility with regard to taxes of this tax base.

Unfortunately, this does not mean that we have discovered a tax whose superiority points inevitably to its introduction as the sole source of revenue. There are many objections to a regime which divides the tax burden equally among the population. To replace all other taxes would require a US Poll tax of $1000 per head or a British poll tax of some £220 per head.

As we saw in chapter 1, the capitalist system produces a very unequal distribution of income and it is considered one of the important functions of government to redress this inequality by subsidizing the poor and the destitute at the expense of the rich members of the community. But a poll tax of any kind would be extremely regressive, and one which raised a large amount of revenue would be impossible for many of the poorer people to pay. There would have to be some exemptions, in which case it would, firstly, no longer be a true poll tax, and, secondly, cause some distortion of the choice between work and leisure to be re-introduced.

The inferiority of selective excise duties on the grounds that excess burdens are imposed is based on the elasticity of demand for the taxed goods with respect to tax. But we saw in chapter 1 that one of the functions of government is to manipulate the consumption of merit and demerit goods by taxes and subsidies (negative taxes). The excess burden argument is conducted as though the optimal choice were always made by a sovereign consumer. But as we also saw in chapter 1, there may be social costs and social benefits of various actions which cause consumers to choose too little or too much of some goods. Again, because of ignorance of the long-run effects of consumption a government medical statistician may be better able to express the consumer's best interests than the consumer can himself. Thus while the consumer may choose to consume large quantities of alcohol at pre-tax prices because the short-run effects are all he cares for, the authorities will be able more coolly to assess the long-run effects on this consumer's well being and that of his immediate family. The British authorities have decided that the undesirable long-run effects of alcohol are on the whole underestimated by consumers and that at pre-tax prices consumption would be higher than was consistent with long-run well being. It is precisely in order to distort consumers' choices that these taxes are imposed. And what of the excess burden of this tax? The presumption is that the tax will give benefits in excess of the excess burden by reducing consumption and so reducing both long-run adverse effects and social costs.

Another case in which the source of the excess burden (elasticity) may be just what is required by social welfare is where monopoly exists. The excess burden proposition depends upon the assumption of perfect competition. The distortion of consumers choices is therefore away from a perfectly competitive optimum. In the case of an imperfect market the distortion of consumers' choices by taxes may just as well move the system towards the competitive optimum. For example a monopolist selling refrigerators will be restricting output below the competitive level and raising price above that which would maintain in perfect competition. If there is full employment the sub-optimal production of one good implies the over-production of at least one other good. Selective excises on non-monopolized products then will raise prices and move the economy towards that allocation of productive capacity which would maintain it in perfect competition.

The excess burden of the poll tax

At the high rates of tax envisaged above, it is doubtful whether the conclusion that the base of a poll tax does not shrink in response to a tax is tenable. Instead, it is likely that, faced with such a poll tax, marriages (which are already postponed for economic reasons) and the having of children would be curtailed. The idea of treating wives and children as economic goods may not be very appealing to many despite the fact that hard choices have to be made in deciding to take a wife, to have another child or to keep a child out of the labour market in order to take higher education. But the introduction of a poll tax which obliged the head of a household to pay £220 or $1000 per head of his family would certainly distort the householder's choices.

In fact the Joseph conclusion can be reversed to show that even a poll tax distorts consumers' choices by distorting the choice between wife and children, and all other goods.

In Figure 20, AB is the pre-tax price line, representing the choice available to an individual between family and other goods. A poll tax of AC per head is introduced, which moves the price line to CE and the consumer's level of satisfaction drops from IC_1 to IC_2. But the same amount of revenue, DA could be raised by an income, excise or any other tax and this would move the consumer's income line to DF. Here the consumer can attain a higher indifference curve IC_3. So a true poll tax imposes an excess burden by distorting the choice between wife and children, and all other goods.

The conclusion must be that all taxes distort choices and that there is no tax that is universally neutral. The excess burdens associated with various taxes will vary in size, but there is no *a priori* way of choosing between these burdens. While it is very likely that choices between other goods and wives and children are not highly susceptible to price changes, it also seems possible that any excess burden arising from a distortion

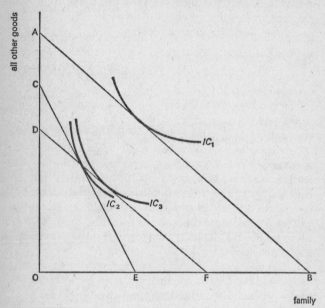

Figure 20

of the choice of family size will have a much more important impact on the consumers well-being than the distortion of his choice between two consumer goods.

Freidman's general equilibrium model established the superior neutrality of income taxes and poll taxes when compared to selective excises, without depending on the assumption of required yield and while taking into account the likelihood of diminishing marginal rates of transformation between goods. But the conclusion in favour of income taxes is still dependent on the assumption that there is a constant supply of effort. This is in many cases an unwarranted assumption.

Little's three dimensional model

Little (1951) has pointed out that one cannot assume that the supply of effort will be the same under both direct and indirect taxes, so that one cannot presume that the income to be divided between consumption of good x and other goods will be the same under both regimes.

Figure 21 is a three dimensional diagram showing that the choice between leisure and work (or money income), and good x. We assume an economy of identical consumers. Each consumer can have a maximum of OC of leisure and not do any work and so earn no income, and he will have no money nor any of good x. He can have no leisure and OA of money or other goods and none of good x, or OB of good x and none of all other goods or a combination of the three.

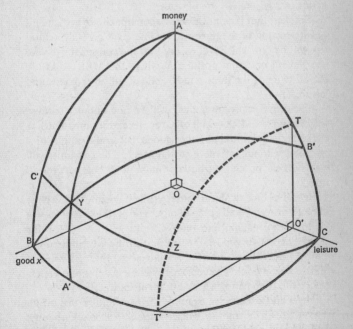

Figure 21

AB is the transformation curve showing the rate of transformation of good x and all other goods. AC is the transformation curve of all other goods or income and leisure. And BC is the transformation curve of good x and leisure. ABC, then, is a full employment production surface after the government's demands upon the country's scarce resources have been made. A'A is the surface line along which the marginal rate of substitution and the marginal rate of transformation of leisure and good x are equal. Along B'B, MRS = MRT, for leisure and money and C'C shows the optimal distribution of any feasible income between good x and other goods, i.e. again the MRT = MRS one for the other. A'A, B'B and C'C describe all possible partial optima. They describe the optimal choices between the relevant pairs of good x, all other goods and leisure.

It is clear that the only general optimum choice is the point of intersection of the three surface lines at Y. A truly neutral tax will be one which will ensure that the consumers achieve the general optimum position Y where the MRS = MRT, for all pairs of the three goods, good x, all other goods and leisure.

A selective excise on good x will be non-optimal because while MRT = MRS for all other goods and leisure, MRS $\neq$ MRT for good x and all other goods, because the price of x is raised without reference to the MRT. The consumer will put himself on the partial optimum B'B but between B and Y.

But an income tax is no better. While it does not disturb the choice between good x and all other goods (the consumer will be in partial equilibrium on C'C with MRS = MRT for good x and other goods), the fact that leisure is subsidized will distort the choices between leisure and other goods, and leisure and good x. The consumer will be in sub-optimal partial equilibrium between Y and C, in this case at Z.

A general excise, for example an expenditure tax on all goods, like an income tax, will leave the choice between good x and other goods undisturbed but will disturb the choice between leisure and good x. If, as we have assumed, savings are constant, a general excise tax, by reducing the purchasing power of income, acts like a proportional income tax.

Summary and conclusion

The neutrality approach to the selection of a tax base has proved incapable of providing us with a unique answer to the problems of selecting the tax base. The poll tax, even if it were truly neutral, is too regressive to be accepted politically and in the case of demerit goods, including imports in times of balance-of-payments difficulties, the very object of taxation is to intervene between the consumer and his first choice. However, neutrality is an important subsidiary consideration.

Where regressiveness is thought tolerable or redistributive tax-subsidy policies have been satisfactorily pursued, and where distortion of the consumer's choice to take account of long-run and social costs and benefits is not the objective, neutrality can be taken into account to reduce the excess burdens of taxation. Several guide rules may be advanced.

1. Capricious taxation should be eliminated. Unless there is a good reason to the contrary, all consumption should be taxed rather than selected types of consumption. All incomes should be taxed with horizontal equality rather than selectively (with different rates for earned income, unearned income and capital gains).

2. As decisions about the production, distribution and exchange of the national income are taken on marginal considerations, taxes should wherever possible avoid falling at the margin. Thus, where possible, and where it does not impose undesirable barriers to entry, it is preferable to sell licences to deal rather than charge duty on each dealing. For example, the marginal cost of using uncongested rural roads is virtually nil, any mileage tax on driving will raise price above marginal cost and cause some people to make stay-at-home decisions when they would otherwise have made a journey. This revenue would have been better raised by a car-licence fee which (although it might discourage some from car ownership) will

leave those who do buy cars to make rational decisions about fully utilizing their cars, and the roads.

3. Taxes should be levied, other things being equal, on tax bases which are inelastic with respect to taxation in order to minimize the extent to which taxation disrupts the working of the market.

4. The debate about whether to tax income or general consumption could not, however, be settled on the basis of which provides the least flexible tax base. The more flexible the base for a general consumption tax, the better, since the general reduction of consumption is the first aim of taxation. On the other hand, if it is ever shown conclusively that income is, as is generally believed, highly flexible with respect to taxation, then the argument for concentrating taxes on consumption would be very greatly strengthened.

Finally, it may be that death-duties are the most neutral taxes as the death rate is likely to remain the same (at one per person) irrespective of the level of death duties. Unfortunately, of course, it is bequests, not deaths, that form the tax base here, and various loopholes exist for avoiding death-duties, thus allowing this tax base a considerable degree of flexibility.

8 The Benefit Approach

The benefit approach to selecting the rates and bases upon which taxation should be levied has two main attractions. The first is that it appeals to many people on grounds that it is fair. Equity is best served, it may be argued, if the beneficiaries of government expenditure pay for these benefits through taxation in proportion as they benefit. This implies extending the principles applying in the private sector to the public sector: the government being analogous to a private firm selling various social and merit goods. The second advantage of the benefit approach is that it gives *simultaneous determination* of the tax level and of the level of government expenditure required. As with the private sector, the prices that people were willing to pay and the amount that they were willing to buy would be determined simultaneously. Thus the problem of how big the public sector should be and, of more operational credibility, how extensive the individual functions of government should be, would be solved at the same time as the problem of who should pay for them.

Three basic models are used in discussing the pure theory of the benefit approach: those of Lindahl, Bowen and Samuelson. Each model determines tax liability on the basis of how much the consumer could be induced to pay by an omniscient despot. Thus tax liability varies with the taxpayers estimate of how much the social goods are worth to him. The taxpayer's willingness to pay is determined by his desire for the social good and by his income – the rich are *ceteris paribus* willing to pay more. To the extent that the rich are willing to pay more for social goods, the benefit approach encompasses an estimate of ability to pay (the other basic approach to allocation of the tax burden; see chapter 9). The benefit approach seeks to ascertain the taxpayer's estimate of his true ability to pay.

The Lindahl (1919) model

This model makes four assumptions. Firstly, that there is one social good; secondly that the social good is enjoyed by two taxpayers, A and B. Thirdly, the distribution of income is ideal. This assumption, though, as we shall see, of great importance for the benefit approach to taxation, is not immediately relevant to the demonstration of simultaneous determination of tax shares and the extent of provision of social goods. And fourthly, that the social good is produced under conditions of constant costs; this assumption, too, is not immediately relevant.

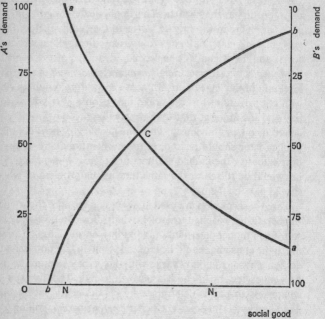

Figure 22

Figure 22 shows the demands of the two consumers A and B for the social good. A's demand curve is shown by aa and bb is B's demand curve. These curves show the percentage of the cost each consumer is willing to pay for a range of outputs of the social good. The social good yields diminishing marginal utility. Thus if ON of social goods were provided, A would be willing to pay all of the cost of providing this good for both A and B. But B would be willing to pay some 85 per cent of the total cost. But if ON_1, of social goods were offered, A would only feel it worth paying 30 per cent of the cost, and B would be willing to pay only 25 per cent. This economy is clearly in equilibrium at C where the willingness of the two consumers to pay for the social good adds up to 100 per cent of the cost of providing the social good.

Thus the Lindahl model gives *simultaneous determination* of the extent of the provision of social goods and of the tax shares of the individuals. The trouble with this model arises when one considers closely the mechanism by which the equilibrium at C is reached.

Musgrave (1959, pp. 78–80) has made four relevant observations. Firstly, that a voting process need not lead to the equilibrium solutions. Secondly, that the output and cost-share problems will have to be decided by a bargaining process and will thus be determined by the skill in negotiation of A and B. Only if there is perfect knowledge or equal skill is C attained. Nevertheless, one may expect negotiation to establish a position somewhere near C. Each may be willing to reveal his preferences more or less truly because in a two-man economy each knows that the other taxpayer must bear the rest of the tax burden. But, thirdly, when you have many consumers, each individual knows his own contribution has a minimal effect on the actual provision of social goods. Indeed, taxation and the provision of social goods becomes quite divorced in the public mind. This is well illustrated by Seldon (1967) whose survey showed that 32–87 per cent (depending on the service in question) of British taxpayers thought there should be more expenditure on the main social services, while 88 per cent thought taxes were already too high. And fourthly, the Lindahl model does not take into account the effects of varying the output of social goods upon this price.

The Bowen (1948) model

The Bowen model is perhaps simpler. It has the virtue of easy adaptation to show what happens under the likely conditions that social goods are produced under conditions of increasing costs; the opportunity costs of private goods foregone. Consider Figure 23.

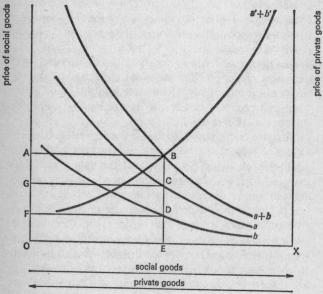

Figure 23

Again we have one social good and two taxpayer-consumers, A and B. The demands of A and B respectively for social goods are represented by a and b, and $a+b$ is the total demand for social goods – the sum of a and b. The supply curve of social goods is represented by $a'+b'$, showing that these goods are produced under conditions of increasing cost. But the cost of producing social goods is the value of the private goods foregone to make their production possible. This means that

$a' + b'$, as well as being the supply curve of social goods, is also the demand curve of private goods.

The intersection of the cost and demand schedules for social goods at B gives us the determination of how a given national income, OX, should, according to the consumer–taxpayers' desires, be divided between the social good and private goods. There should be OE of the social goods and EX of private goods.

But simultaneously the tax shares of A and B are determined according to the consumers' own valuation of the benefits they receive from social goods. The total tax requirement is represented by area ABEO in Figure 23. The shares of A and B are found by reference to a and b. At that level of provision of social goods, A is willing to pay GCEO and B is willing to pay FDEO. But ABEO = GCEO + FDEO. Musgrave (1966, 1969) favours the Bowen model because of its easy generalization of the real world.

In an economy of consumer/taxpayers, the demand for social goods is computed by adding individual demand schedules, and the tax liability is read off each individual demand schedule.

Samuelson's pure theory (1954, 1955, 1958, 1969)

Samuelson's work on the pure theory of public expenditures puts the problem of allocating tax shares in a general equilibrium framework, using the techniques of the new welfare economics. This is designed to avoid two problems associated with the work described so far:

1. It avoids the problem of revealed preference. It is all right for Bowen and Lindahl to talk about consumers revealing preferences in a two-person economy. But as we have seen in chapter 1, the revealing of such preferences in the real world is only plausible where the exclusion principle is applied.

2. It avoids the difficulty associated at least with the Lindahl model that it gives only a partial solution. It deals with the provision of social goods as though this were independent of the provision for private goods.

Samuelson considers the optimal choice between 'a private consumption good, like bread' and 'a public consumption good, like an outdoor circus or national defense', in a two-man economy. Figure 24 (a) shows the transformation curve of the private into the social good and (b) and (c) are the indifference maps of two individuals showing how they would choose between these goods. The nation's output of private goods is shared between the two but the social good is consumed equally by both. This means that the horizontal scale in all three diagrams is equal; that any output of social goods (OM) is consumed equally by the two individuals.

If OM of social goods is produced, we see from (a) that only ME of private goods is available for consumption by either individual 1 or 2. There are an infinite number of ways that the private goods may be divided. What we now have to do is to describe all the efficient distributions of the private goods between consumers 1 and 2. We need to identify all those distributions on which it is impossible to improve the position of one consumer without making the other worse off – the Pareto-optima.

Let us set man 1 on indifference curve U_2. How high an indifference curve is it then possible for man 2 to get on?

Assume social goods OM. An amount ME private goods is therefore to be divided between 1 and 2. Therefore to be on U_2 man 1 must get ME' of private goods. This leaves ME'' available for man 2, who then attains his highest possible indifference curve U'_2.

Samuelson derives the Pareto-optima in the following way. Take U_2 and plot it on Figure 24 (d). This will give man 1's private consumption. The difference between U_2 and the transformation curve will show the possibilities open to man 2 while man 1 is on U_2. So subtract U_2 from AB and plot on man 2's indifference map as in Figure 24 (e), giving the point where the U_2 is tangent to U'_2. There are an infinite number of these Pareto-optima each one corresponding to a different initial choice of indifference curve of man 1.

Figure 25 shows the utility of man 1 on the horizontal axis and that of man 2 on the vertical axis. PP is a utility frontier

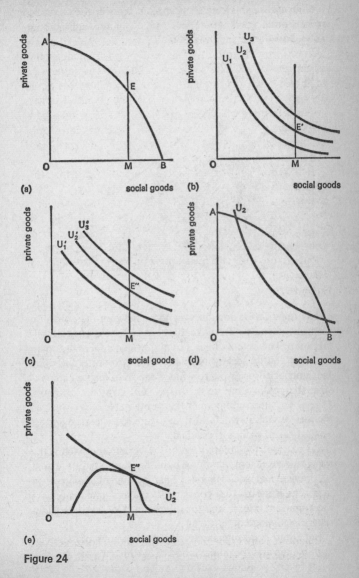

(a)

private goods
social goods

(b)

private goods
social goods

(c)

private goods
social goods

(d)

private goods
social goods

(e)

private goods
social goods

Figure 24

along which all the Pareto-optima are plotted. All points to the north-east are unattainable levels of welfare and all those in the shaded area are sub-optimal.

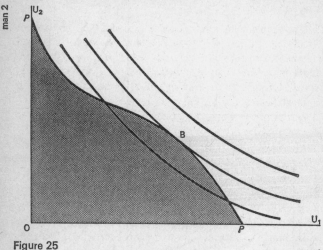

Figure 25

The question is: how do we choose between the points on the utility frontier? To make this choice we need a social welfare map. This is an indifference map which applies not to an individual but to society as a whole. It incorporates the value judgements of society as to what is the good life and emphasizes the political nature of this type of economic decision. Clearly the super-optimum or 'best obtainable bliss point', as Samuelson calls it, will be at B on Figure 25, where the highest level of social welfare is reached.

To sum up: the great virtue of the benefit approach is the simultaneous determination of both tax shares and the extent of provision of social goods. This is thought desirable by many, as it means that consumer-taxpayers' preferences are the important criteria and the discretion of political decision-takers is eliminated.

But Samuelson emphasizes the political nature of the social welfare map and the unlikelihood of reaching the highest bliss point by any voluntary exchange system because of the problem of revealed preference. However it is when we come to consider the general application of the benefit approach to taxation that we come up against a formidable list of difficulties. Among these are:

1. The problems of getting people to reveal their preferences accurately. In the two-person economy, preference may well be revealed by self-interested individuals. But when there are many taxpayers and preferences it will pay people to understate their preferences, as a reduction in their payments will not significantly reduce the provision of social goods. If preferences are not revealed they must be guessed, which leaves the authorities with a lot of discretionary power.

2. Consumers may be ignorant of benefits and so not be able to reveal all their preferences. Many of the benefits of public expenditures give rise to externalities. How are people to reveal their total preferences for education when they are unlikely to appreciate (let alone to care about) how much benefit they confer on others by their literacy? The value of literacy to the individual is a function of how many other literates there are with whom he can communicate.

3. As Arrow (1963) has pointed out, even if all preferences were revealed willingly it would still be possible to derive a social welfare function only if there is transivity between choices. In the real world intransitivity is likely; different individuals will rank the various choices open to them differently.

4. The benefit rule cannot provide a universal rule of taxation if we accept that the government has to support the poor. There will always be some people who would earn nothing in a free market and many more who would earn amounts which would be considered inadequate on humanitarian grounds. These people have to be given income and this must be paid for by taxation (of those who have higher incomes) according to some other principle than that of benefit.

It can be argued that the rich derive benefits from redistribution (see chapter 11), but the point here is that the benefits accruing to the poor as a result of redistribution cannot, by definition, be subjected to taxation.

5. The benefit rule cannot deal with the problems of stabilization which are so important in forming current fiscal policy. For example, if an economy has a chronic tendency to unemployment, as it seemed in the 1930s all capitalist countries had, then government expenditure will be required to exceed government revenue permanently so as permanently to raise effective demand. A system of simultaneous determination of expenditure and at a level equal to what taxpayers were willing to pay would not be capable of providing the functional finance answer to this problem. At least there would have to be some benefits which were not matched by taxation. The government would have, for example, to print money and distribute it to increase effective demand.

We have introduced the three pioneering models still used in discussing the benefit approach. Those who wish to pursue this further should consult Johanson (1963) and Musgrave (1966) where the Lindahl model is refined, Samuelson (1969) for his latest thoughts on the model described here, McGuire and Aaron (1969) who claim that 'the foregoing analysis effectively completes the destruction of the benefit principle as a practical foundation for the determination of tax shares for the production of public goods except under special circumstances', and Musgrave (1966, 1969) where he, like the present author, favours the Bowen approach as having the most operational significance.

The benefit approach and economic policy

The benefit theory finds practical expression in the regimes proposed by the liberal economists whose views are often identified with the University of Chicago in the United States and whose work forms the bulk of the published output of the British Institute of Economic Affairs. Perhaps the best known statement of the liberal position is contained in Friedman and Friedman (1962). It is assumed that on the whole consumers are rational and that given the freedom to exercise choice they will choose exactly what they want. Governments are not in a position to know better than individuals what individuals want. It is highly dangerous to let the public sector grow because this means a growth in that part of the national income which is not allocated according to consumers' choices.

The connection of the liberals with the benefit approach to taxation lies in the fact that the benefit approach would mirror consumer choices giving simultaneous determination of tax shares and the amount of goods to be provided as does the market. It is accepted that the benefit principle cannot be applied to all government activity because of the problems listed on pages 107–8 but a rational system of simultaneous determination is so important that wherever possible provision of goods and services should be made outside the public sector and that, where goods and services of a marketable nature are provided by state agencies they should be sold – not given away. Earmarked taxes should be used where possible. Thus public expenditure on roads could be financed from an earmarked tax on car ownership. This would be fair as the beneficiaries of roads would pay for their upkeep. It would also tend to give a rational 'output' of roads because road users who found road space or quality inadequate and who knew that their taxes would be earmarked for road improvement and nothing else would be in a position to express a genuine choice of how much should be spent on roads. In the absence of earmarking, motorists will always favour *lower* road taxes and *higher* expenditure on roads. In this way the maximum degree of payment by beneficiaries is achieved: the maximum degree of identity between consumer preferences and provision of goods and services is achieved.

The extreme liberal approach would prescribe a regime in which all marketable goods and services were provided by the private sector. The state would provide only the pure social goods, such as national defence and the legal system, which cannot be traded because the exclusion principle cannot be applied. Urban parks might be provided by the state as it would be too costly to exclude anyone from their use, but national parks can be put to a market test by charging for entry. Those who are unwilling to pay will reveal their lack of interest in national parks and be excluded. There would be no merit goods like medicine, state education and state-run, subsidized, or compulsory insurance for retirement, for example. An extreme liberal regime would now allow the state to intervene in the market to pursue the objectives of stabilization or redistribution of income or wealth.

Perhaps it is not surprising that even the extreme liberals are not that extreme. All the difficulties of applying a pure benefit regime mentioned on pages 107–8 are recognized to greater or lesser extent.

Turning over a larger part of the economy to private enterprise would still leave the taxation problems associated with stabilization to be tackled. Few would deny that the old pre-Keynesian concept of a neutral budget with revenue balancing expenditure without reference to employment and inflation is out of date in 1968. Even Friedman has said, 'We are all Keynesians now'; but nevertheless there is a section of liberal opinion led by the Chicago monetary school which believes that a far less active stabilization policy is required of government taxation and that the great burden of macroeconomic control should be borne by monetary policy. The controversy about the relative importance of fiscal and monetary policy is outside the scope of this volume, but it does seem that an over-active fiscal policy may have had a somewhat destabilizing influence in Great Britain in the 1950s and 1960s and that until 1969 too little attention was paid to the influence of the supply of money on demand. However, there is no doubt that the authorities in Britain and America see fiscal policy as being very much concerned with stabilization.

The problem of distribution is recognized by the Liberals. The state must provide for those who in a true market economy would receive an intolerably low income. It is a proper function of governments to provide for the poor and tax the rest of the community to pay for such provision. However, it is the Liberals' assertion that such support of the poor should come, not in the form of social services provided free, but in the form of cash. This belief is based on the welfare assumption that the recipient must be at least as well off getting the cash as getting medical treatment, etc., because if it is medical treatment he wants then he will buy medical insurance and be as well off as if medical insurance were free. But if the consumer prefers to spend his money on a better house or on whisky then he will do so and be better off. The consumer will choose freely those goods which he wants most and so, being rational and best able to know what he wants, will optimize the content of his share of the national income.

The existence of externalities is also recognized by the liberals as a valid reason for government provision or subsidization of various activities. The trouble with external costs and benefits is that they are very difficult to measure with any accuracy. This means that a great deal of power is placed in the hands of the cost-benefit engineer or the political decision-maker to interpret the evidence wrongly. The suspicions of the liberals are well expressed by Lord Robbins (oddly enough, as the Robbins Report on higher education stresses most strongly the importance and magnitude of the external benefits of education):

But important as this argument may be in particular cases, it is easy to see how frightfully it may be abused as a justification for general paternalism. There is scarcely anything I do outside the privacy of my home which has not some overtone of indiscriminate benefit or detriment. The clothes I wear, the shows I frequent, the flowers I plant in my garden, all directly, or through the mysterious influence of fashion, influence the enjoyments and satisfactions of others. The fact that other people lead a way of life different from my own, that they like and buy pictures and books of which I disapprove, and give private banquets of sacred meats and forbidden wines, can clearly be the occasion to me of the most intense mortification. Is this to be included in the calculus of external economies and diseconomies? I can think of few forms of totalitarian regimentation of consumption which could not find some formal justification by appeal to this analysis (Robbins, 1947, pp. 20–21).

Therefore extreme caution should be exercised in deciding how much socialization to justify on the grounds that important externalities exist. Three rules are implicit in the liberal approach. Firstly, that public intervention in the market on the grounds that externalities exist is only justified if these externalities can be clearly shown to exist and are very substantial. Small gains from public intervention are not worth the erosion or threat of erosion of freedom of choice. Secondly, that no other activities be taken into the public sector just because associated activities have externalities associated with them. Education may yield external benefits to the community as a whole but liberals believe one should not make that an excuse for providing state schools with swimming pools or music teachers. It is the three Rs that give the externalities. Frills like singing lessons yield only private benefits and should be paid for by the singer not the taxpayer. And thirdly, that the externalities be externalities in which a trade-off is not possible between the receivers of social costs and benefits and the people engaged in the economic activity in question as consumers and producers.

The logical outcome of the liberal approach with its concentration on market forces wherever possible is a very small public sector and a smaller tax bill. Friedman has listed some of the activities undertaken by the government of the most market orientated economy of the world, the United States, which he believes it improper for a government to undertake. These include rent control, wage control and price control. Minimum wage legislation, manipulation of interest rates, subsidies, conscription in peace time (wages should just be raised until the army is staffed), subsidies, for example, for slum clearance or social security programs which force one to save. The government should not regulate commerce, impose tariff quotas or other trade restrictions, issue licences or control radio and television as it does through the Federal Communications Commission. The state should not seek to provide national parks or run a state monopolized post office nor should there be publicily operated toll roads. Friedman says this list is far from complete.

It should be noted that not all of these government functions give rise to a tax bill. The denationalization of the post office, for example, would cut the British government's revenue from profits. And if the nationalized post office were replaced by a lot of wastefully-competitive private firms this might set up inflationary pressures which would necessitate further increases in taxes.

There is no doubt that Friedman would find a lot more to put on his list if he looked at the economy of the United Kingdom. And indeed a good deal of interesting work has recently been done by members of the Institute of Economic Affairs, showing why and how liberal principles might be applied to various sectors of Britain's welfare machinery. We shall look at some of these now.

Buchanan (1966) and Lees (1961) on health

In Britain the National Health Service is available to all and maintained by taxation as defined on page 24, chapter 2. Lees believes that this system should be changed to a system of private insurance and private enterprise. Tax-financed medicine is less efficient than marketed medicine on several counts. There is over-consumption of some medical services because no account is taken by the consumer of the cost and this leads to queueing which wastes everyone's time. There is less spent on medicine in Britain than in many other countries because people are not given the chance through the price mechanism to express the true extent of their choice as consumers of medical services. This means consumers get a lower quality of service than that for which they would be willing to pay in a market economy.

The rest of Lees's case for marketed medicine lies in the weaknesses of the case for socialized medicine. The socialist case he sees as having five points:

1. The first is that health services, being a necessity of life, should not be made subject to private profit. The unequal struggle between Dr Entrepreneur and Mr Sick is regarded as uncivilized. This is a value judgement about which the economist as such cannot say much. Except to observe as Lees does that health services are certainly no more a necessity of life than food and also that the mechanism of payment would normally be through insurance, the payments for which would be made while people were fit.

2. The case for socialized medicine stresses the importance of externalities. Lees points out that the great bulk of medical expenditure concerns, not contagious disease where externalities are obviously important, but rheumatism, accidents and non-contagious complaints like appendicitis where the benefits are quite private. Most of the contagious diseases involve control measures: questions of public health rather than of medicine. At any rate only an estimated 5 per cent of medical expenditure can be justified on grounds of external benefits of disease prevention.

3. Socialists believe that the great income inequality in a market economy would lead to a very unequal distribution of medical treatment and that this would be undesirable. Lees points out (a) that this is an ethical not an economic problem and, (b) that it is a red herring. This is essentially a problem of income inequality and has nothing to do with medicine. The state should take such steps as are thought necessary to equalize incomes and then leave people to spend their incomes on health services or other goods as they see fit.

4. The socialist fear that ignorance will lead to under-provision of private medical insurance is dismissed as implausible. At any rate in so far as ignorance is a problem the rational thing to do is to remove ignorance by encouraging information services. It is not a sensible policy to treat a disease (ignorance) by treating a symptom (under insurance).

5. It has been argued by protagonists of tax-financed medicine, including the Webbs, that medical expenditure is not only health-producing but wealth-producing; a healthy society will be able to work harder and fewer days will be lost due to illness. Lees points out that while improved health was undoubtedly important in advanced countries in the early stages of economic development, there is little scope for wealth production through health expenditure in the 1960s. Even if days lost through illness could be eliminated by medical advance, there would only be an increase in days worked of 0·5 per cent. Indeed, health expenditure may be increasingly wealth-

consuming as, in the age of spare-part surgery and antibiotics, the principal achievements of medical science and medical care are the extension of the length of the non-working life. An ageing population is likely to be less productive per man.

Buchanan describes the malaise of the British health service as consisting of under-supply, characterized by staff shortages and a low standard of amenity, and excess-demand causing queueing. This is caused fundamentally by the lack of simultaneous determination of medical-service benefits and the amount consumers have to pay for such services. There is a basic contradiction (in the provision of free services by the state) between the determinants of demand and the determinants of supply.

On the demand side it is impossible for 'free' services to lead to anything but an excessive level of demand. In Figure 26(a), S is a supply curve of medical services showing the long-run marginal cost of such services, and D is the demand for medical care. This demand curve may be taken to represent the demand for medical services which would obtain after a desired distribution of income had been attained and if perfect knowledge was general.

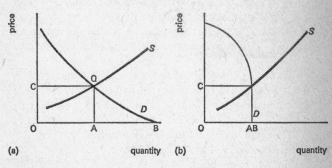

Figure 26

The amount of medical service provided in a free market would be OA at a price OC. But under a system of state provision of free services, OB will be required by consumers at the zero price. This represents an over-supply of AB because the consumers of this amount of treatment are not willing to pay the real cost of such treatment.

Thus the quantity demanded is augmented by free medicine, except in the case of Figure 26 (b), where demand is quite inelastic over the relevant range. Buchanan believes that demand for most medical services would be elastic.

The quantity supplied on the other hand will tend to be reduced under a system of provision through taxes. In a free market, the quantity supplied is fixed at the point at which no consumer is willing to pay for a further increment of treatment. The same is true under a system of state provision though the mechanism of payment is different. In a free market payment by the consumer is made direct to the producer. With state medicine the consumer states his preference through the ballot box and makes payment in taxes to the government of his democratic choice. Ignoring for the moment the inexactness of this process for reflecting individual consumers preferences, there is every reason to expect, on *a priori* grounds, that the willingness of consumers to pay via taxation will be less than under a market system. This is because whereas in a market, the consumer himself enjoys the benefits of his expenditure, in the case of state health services the consumer-taxpayer is asked to consider medical expenditure the benefits of which will be felt by all people in the economy.

This finding is to some extent supported by opinion polls which show that people think that the level of provision of medical services is too low but that the tax bill is too high.

Thus the provision of free health (and other) services is bound to lead to reduced supply and increased demand. The deficiencies observed in the health services are deemed by Buchanan to be predictable and a direct result of the system of state provision.

Peacock and Wiseman (1964) on education

The inadequacies of a system of free state provision are believed likely to be more or less evident in all social services. It is not surprising, given the extent of government expenditure on education in advanced countries, that liberals have produced a variety of schemes for organizing and reorganizing such state expenditures. One interesting contribution among many is the program for progressive liberalization of the British education system proposed by Peacock and Wiseman.

The undesirable features of state provision which it is desired to eliminate are:

1. As with health expenditures under-supply which is produced by the unwillingness of taxpayers to vote sufficient finance. Symptoms are low teacher-salaries leading to staff-shortages and teacher-unrest.

2. The lack of an effective range of choice within the state system. There is simply a public sector which is 'free', and a private sector which is so expensive that only a very small proportion of parents can afford to send their children there. Most people having decided where to live have little or no choice in education.

3. The state schools tend to aim for homogeneity. This frustrates the willingness to experiment with different teaching and organizational methods, and so inhibits the advance of educational ideas.

4. The lack of parental choice produces a lack of parental interest and general ignorance of education methods and objectives.

5. The lack of competition means there is little impetus to cost-saving or improving the excellence of the product.

Much of the paternalist case is seen to be weak or more compatible with other systems of educational organization than with state provision. Externalities accruing as a result of education of the individual to society as a whole may be exaggerated. Peacock and Wiseman suspect that the recipients of education may appropriate most of such benefits in the form of higher wages and salaries. Ignorance of the important issues at stake in the choice of education are seen as unimportant in advanced economies. The poor in an illiterate society may have to have all decisions taken out of their hands because they are not equipped to make such decisions, but in advanced countries people are on the whole capable of making such choices. The fact that some may be too poor to spend their money on education is an argument against poverty, not against private provision of educational facilities. What is required is measures to redistribute capital and income, not the provision of free education. It may be necessary in the United States, for example, to provide state-financed and state-run schooling in order to get the American way of life spread among the various immigrant populations: it may be necessary to use the education system to produce social cohesion. This is not really necessary in Britain although such measures of state provision may be desirable in those areas in which African and Asian immigration is concentrated.

The class divisions of society may be perpetuated to some extent by a system in which there is choice in education. But abolishing choice is not the only way to overcome the difficulty. Peacock and Wiseman envisage a whole range of educational opportunities and expenditures as becoming possible. This would replace the present two-tier system in Britain with a continuous range. Instead of two classes, one paying for education and one getting it free, there would be a continuous gradation which would make class distinction harder to maintain and class mobility more likely.

However, some considerable state intervention in the provision of education is recognized as necessary and seven *agreed objectives* of such intervention are listed:

1. To ensure a minimum universal education. Education must be made compulsory and the state must supervise the standard of such education.

2. To contribute finance to ensure that the benefits of literacy continue to be enjoyed by society.

3. To contribute to the finance of higher education which provides external benefits, including the supply of teachers with which society is thus provided.

4. In order to ensure that no talent is wasted through lack of

funds, the state should ensure that adequate loan finance is available to undergraduates to pay such fees (and maintenance allowances) as are required to augment the state contribution to higher education.

5. To control monopoly elements in education as in the rest of society.

6. To provide information services to aid individuals in the exercise of choice.

7. To take into account such social objectives as are highly desired by society.

Peacock and Wiseman's 'ideal policy for a developed democracy'

The state would supervise the standards of, and make compulsory, primary education but would not provide education. The state would no longer own or run schools and colleges. Ownership of educational institutes would pass to a variety of private and public bodies who would be independent of the state and would be run as independent bodies deriving their incomes from fees. Parents would receive a voucher in respect of each child to the value of a minimum acceptable level of education. With this voucher they would purchase education at the school of their choice. Parents who wanted a higher standard of education for their children would be able to supplement the value of their vouchers and send their children to more expensive schools. It is anticipated that a wide range of expensive and cheap schools would arise offering very different kinds of service between which parents would choose.

Vouchers would also be provided to cover part only of the cost of higher education. These could be presented in part payment of University fees and supplemented out of parental incomes or bursaries etc., or by borrowing from a government-sponsored body. These loans would be paid back out of the students' future income.

These reforms would lead to a big increase in expenditure on education. The building programme would be increased and staff shortages would be ended by raising salaries. Choice would be general and academic freedom enhanced. The student would now have to borrow in order to invest in education just like the shopkeeper who borrows to buy his stock. The uneducated labourer would no longer be taxed to pay for the education of the solicitor.

Roth on roads (1966)

In Britain and the United States road use is normally free. Some tolls are levied but normally the roads are made available as social services and paid for out of general taxation. It is true that many taxes are levied on motorists – but these are not normally earmarked for paying the costs of running the road network. Licence fees and sales taxes are in no obvious way connected with the extent of road use, and even petrol tax payments, though they do reflect the mileage covered, do not distinguish between the use of scarce crowded urban roads and plentiful rural road space.

Road taxes are therefore no help in equilibrating the demand and supply of road space. Even when tolls are levied they are usually designed to produce revenue rather than to optimize resource allocation. It is common for tolls to be abandoned when, e.g. the bridge has paid for itself. Roth suggests we treat road space like any other commodity and establish a market in mileage. This would give simultaneous determination of who pays road taxes and how much they pay, and where to spend money on roads and how much to spend.

Equilibrium in the mileage market

The market is said to be in equilibrium when the marginal cost of journeys is equal to the average revenue: when price = MC = AR.

Fixed costs

The operation of a road involves certain fixed costs. Rent of land used, interest on capital employed in construction, and maintenance made necessary by wear and tear caused by the elements.

Marginal costs

Then there are the marginal costs which are the important costs from the point of view of market equilibrium. The marginal cost according to Roth has four components:

1. Private costs. There are the costs to motorists of petrol, wear and tear on their cars, and time.

2. Road-use costs include wear and tear inflicted upon the road by the vehicle in question and the street-lighting, traffic-lights, and police-time necessary to the successful operation of the road.

3. Congestion costs. These are external costs inflicted upon road users by other road users. If another car enters a crowded street it inflicts costs on all other motorists in the street. These costs are in the form of time wasted and some extra running costs not to mention the extremely important but hard to estimate cost of wear and tear on the nerves.

Table 11 shows the effect on the costs of other motorists of another car joining a traffic stream travelling at various speeds. If the traffic is moving at 20 m.p.h. and another car enters the stream of traffic, this will cause external costs to those already in the traffic of a total of 2·1p per mile. At eight miles per hour the congestion costs caused by an extra car are 30p per mile, and it is easy to see that if he had to pay the external cost this motorist might be persuaded to stay at home or travel later.

It is in taking into account congestion costs that the greatest gain is to be had from a proper pricing system. With free roads, congestion costs are not taken into account and (as with health

Table 11

Speed of traffic	Congestion cost per mile inflicted by marginal car
20 m.p.h.	2·1p
14 m.p.h.	6·7p
8 m.p.h.	30p

Source: 'Road Pricing: The Economic and Technical Possibilities', HMSO, 1964.

services and education) demand becomes excessive and more people crowd the streets than would do so if they had to pay the full cost of travel.

4. Community costs are other externalities caused by transport. These include damage to the quality of life and so to property values, for example, arising from such things as noise, fumes and danger to residents, inflicted on the surrounding countryside by roads and road traffic. Roth finds such costs too difficult for a road pricing system to deal with and would leave such decisions in the paternalistic hands of the town planners and the political policymakers.

So that an efficient pricing system would make price equal to marginal cost (he calls it user cost) defined as private cost plus use cost plus congestion cost.

The plan of action

Private costs are already borne by the vehicle owner and no new policy is needed here. The road-user costs do not vary very much with road conditions and could be covered by a petrol duty of 4·16p per gallon. Congestion costs would be collected by changing the flat rate licence fee to the 'meter system'.

Instead of buying a year's licence for his car, the motorist would buy a battery which would be fitted to a meter in his vehicle. As the car was driven the battery would discharge and it would be an offence to drive with an uncharged meter. The mechanism of discharge of the batteries would be a series of pricing points. These would be devices set into the road which would cause the discharge of current from the battery. On uncongested rural roads few if any such points would be in operation whereas in congested and/or urban roads there would be many such pricing points. These points would contain up to fifteen dischargers, any number of which could be in operation at once depending on the traffic conditions. At rush hours in London and New York all pricing points would be fully active encouraging marginal users to relieve congestion by bringing forward or postponing journeys. At such times bypasses would be more fully used. Firms would consider making deliveries by night. Commuters might consider doubling up in cars or making fuller use of public transport. On the other hand, motoring in the country would become cheaper.

The cost of introducing such a system in 1964 would have been £5–£15 per meter and £5m for pricing points. The Smead Committee estimated savings to motorists from reduced congestion at £100–£150m per annum.

As marginal costs rise steeply, profits would be made on congested roads showing the need for further expenditure and this expenditure would be borne by those who found it profitable to travel despite having to pay congestion costs. There would be simultaneous determination of who paid for roads, and where and how much to spend on them.

Roth would go further and allow competition in the private provision of rural roads in order further to mirror the market mechanism and to avoid the problems of monopoly.

A case for state provision

What are believers in social services to do in the face of all this economic argument, all this sound and consistent reasoning? They may counter-attack along four lines. Firstly, they may disagree with the Liberals' guesses as to the facts – the elasticity of demand for health services and the importance of externalities for example. Secondly, they may point out weaknesses in particular aspects of Liberal policy; thirdly, they can show how Liberal objectives may be achieved within the system of state provision, and finally, they are entitled to say that in their value judgement there are some areas of economic life in which state provision is more appropriate than market provision, and leave it at that.

We will start with that line of Socialist counter-attack which attempts to dispute the 'facts', not because this is necessarily the most important line, but because it is the one which economists are best qualified to pursue.

Firstly, there is the importance of externalities. Buchanan's analysis of the inevitability of disequilibrium with free state provision ignores the problem of externalities. It may be that when externalities are taken into account optimal allocation is achieved by zero pricing as in Figure 27 (a), or indeed that even zero prices are not low enough, as in Figure 27 (b), where zero pricing produces output OA, whereas private and social benefits taken together would suggest an optimum supply of OB.

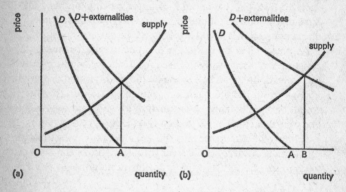

Figure 27

Everyone will agree that strenuous efforts should be made to measure externalities, but liberals will say that when evidence is short it is better to assume externalities away. Paternalists will prefer to err on the side of over-estimating external benefits. There is not much we can say here about the choice between the two approaches except to say, firstly, that there is nothing to choose between them; there is no reason why the onus of proof should lie with either side; and, secondly, that one should try in each case to make one's own guess as to the value of externalities without any pre-disposition.

One genus of externality which may be of great importance but which is seldom mentioned might be added to the socialist case. It is possible to derive considerable benefits from the existence of goods and services without actually using them. There are the benefits which accrue to all the citizens of a society as a result of the knowledge that all the others are being looked after as regards the social service in question. It is of great benefit to me to know that all the poorer people in society will be treated when they are ill and given money when they retire. I may derive external benefits in the form of pride of living in the 'good society' where education is general. Moreover, it is possible to derive external benefits from all sorts of activities without direct consumption. The author derives external benefits from the existence of state subsidized opera and orchestras even though he never actually goes to the theatre. It is certainly worth some money to me to keep the loss-making highland railways open even though I travel everywhere by car. The availability of free health services gives external benefits to the healthy in the form of security in the knowledge that if they break a leg they can have it repaired. If these services are there my options are open and this gives me satisfaction. This type of externality cannot be dismissed as value judgement. The benefits may arise from value judgements about the 'good society', but they are no less real for that.

Liberals will ask if I would not under a system of private provision be willing to contribute voluntarily to charitable institutions which would provide these services. The answer is that I would not because these benefits cannot be made liable to the exclusion principle. I know that my contribution will not make a significant impact on the quality of society. The benefits of my contribution will not be exclusively mine. It is only if everyone is forced to contribute that a real step can be made towards the good society.

Secondly, the liberal argument noted on page 110, that people offered the alternative of one hundred pounds or one hundred pounds worth of social services will always be at least as well off with the money, is open to question. The rationale behind this presumption is that if it is social services that the individual wants he can use the one hundred pounds to buy such services and be as well off as if they were free. If he does not want them he can spend his money on something he values more highly. This, the Liberals say, will mean the individual will be better off with money. A truly benevolent society would not provide free medicine and public parks but would redistribute income so that everyone could afford these services *if they wanted to*. The individual, it is argued, knows better than the state what is good for him. While great weight will be given to this argument by economists, there are grounds for thinking that this rule will not always apply.

There is the problem that with services like education and health insurance the payment and the receipt of benefits may be widely separated in time or in the people they affect. Thus if parents are left to pay the whole cost of educating their children they may prove to be less 'paternalistic' than the state. After all, the benefits may be all the childrens', whereas the payments are all made by the parents. Parental love and pride will often overcome this difficulty but there are plenty of cases where such love is lacking. And we can hardly expect much opposition from the children if parents decline to subject them to academic training.

There is also the problem of parental ignorance. The decision to take out sufficient health insurance has to be taken when one is healthy and it is very easy to be over-optimistic about one's prospects of remaining healthy. The choice between current consumption and protection against unforeseen disasters is one in which the temptations all lie on the side of under-insurance. Liberals will say that the choice belongs to the individual and he will choose at least as well as the state can choose for him. But it may be that civil servants objectively assessing the actuarial tables and fully cognizant of all the medical special disabilities that can befall a man may in fact be able to make a better choice than the individual faced with the choice between a new car and treatment at some unspecified time in the future for disease he hasn't got, hasn't even heard of and may never get.

Thirdly, there is the problem of contract costs – the costs of operating price systems. One of these costs is the cost (trouble) of decision making. One may suspect the assertion that to give money is always best by noticing the special nature of the benefits of receiving presents. Is it really best to send the money and let the recipient buy what he likes? Do the members of the I E A send one another small cheques at Christmas – after all if the recipients like Christmas cards they can use the cheques to buy their own? If not they can spend the money on something which gives them more pleasure, surely? It is very pleasant to get a present rather than money because one is relieved of the decision; contract costs are avoided.

It may confer similar benefits upon the subjects of a paternalistic regime not to have to worry about deciding how much to put away for retirement or how much to spend on medical insurance. An indication that this is important is given by the extent to which wage-earners choose to have prior changes on their incomes (like savings) deducted by their employers rather than make a weekly decision.

Other contract costs include the people employed in sending out bills, receiving the money, making price policy, chasing bad debts, and so on. These contract costs may on occasions be too high to make it worth having a pricing system. Toll collection on quiet roads for example may not be enough to pay the gateman's wages.

A fourth line of socialist counter attack is to dispute the 'facts' about the shape of the demand for the social services in question. We saw on page 115 Buchanan's demonstration that the benefits of a pricing system are to be had if there is elastic demand for such services. The less elastic demand is, the less strong the case for market provision.

The elasticity of demand for a product is a function not only of price but of the prices and closeness of substitutes. It seems likely that Buchanan and Lees have given insufficient consideration to the availability of substitutes. The price system is vital to the functioning of the food market, for example. Here it ensures a ready supply of all goods by making the scarce commodities expensive and the plentiful ones cheap. People choose their diet to fit their incomes. People cannot choose their diseases in quite the same way. If meat were free everyone would demand the most expensive cuts. But a man with a bunion is not likely to ask for neuro-surgery just because he can get this service free.

There are many ways of treating hunger but there is only one cure for a burst appendix. So unless the patient is to be allowed to suffer (and Lees at least would favour fall-back arrangements for those improvident enough to run out of insurance), there is little effective choice of treatment of a wide range of medical complaints. To this extent demand is inelastic.

Of course there are respects in which demand is sensitive to price changes and where a pricing system becomes more appropriate. Plastic surgery, the removal of facial hair and the treatment of hangovers can be undertaken to varying degrees or not at all. The demand for drugs in Britain has shown itself to be highly elastic to a change in price from zero to 12·5p per item on prescription. Then a pricing system is quite appropriate to the decisions on how comfortable and perhaps how long one's stay in hospital should be. The demand for single rooms is likely to be price elastic.

Paternalists would be prepared to argue on efficiency grounds that medical skill should be allocated on the basis of sending the best men to the most difficult cases rather than, as would certainly happen in a market system, to the highest bidder. One might not want the great surgeons of the world to spend much time on millionaire appendectomies.

Then there is Friedman's recommendation that because, while they are undoubtedly important in education externalities stem from literacy and numeracy not from fringe activities like singing and playing games, subsidization should be of education alone. That fringe activities should be paid for by the parents of those who enjoy the activities, is open to question. There are no doubt sociologists who believe that a more complete education provides external benefits in the form of, for example, a more diligent and more law abiding community. There will be doctors who say that attractive hospitals are important to medical cure and cannot be separated from the scalpel and the drug.

Then it is possible to resist the liberal line by attacking weak points in their work. For example Lees asserts that under-provision of medical insurance is unlikely, whereas President Nixon's 1971 State of the Union Message shows that the experience of the United States suggests that widespread under-insurance is possible and does occur. In support of the view that health expenditure is not significantly wealth-producing he alludes to the small number of working days lost through ill health but does not mention the effects on productivity of imperfect health which does not lead to absence from work.

Lees and Buchanan both say that if people cannot afford medical services then efficiency requires us to treat poverty not ill-health. The incomes of the poor should be raised so that they can buy medical insurance if they want to. The advantage of this is that they can choose not to spend on health.

The benefit approach to taxation is based on an excessively naïve concept of the utility function of the individual. Thus utility is made a function of one's own income only. Thus one gets the most efficient use of income when the individual chooses the real goods of which his own income is composed. But as Hochman and Rogers (1969) have shown, utility is also a function of other people's incomes, that is, the rich may actually prefer to give some income to the poor. In societies where the rich are taxed to provide things for the poor it is not accurate to say that the poor get all the benefits of spending their incomes and can therefore choose the goods which produce most benefit. It is quite certain that some of the rich, who may be pleased to be taxed to provide education, will be outraged if the poor are given cash and then choose whisky. If the rich want to benefit by supporting the poor in education and health, then, except in the unlikely case where the poor have a marginal propensity to consume these goods of one, it will be much cheaper to provide the services than to hand out cash – an extremely important point of political economy.

Liberals expect private information services to arise to cope with the complex problems of choice in education and health, though it is recognized that information is likely to be suboptimal in free markets and that government provision or subsidization of information services may be necessary. Paternalists are free to question whether agencies of sufficient quality can be set up to counter the degree of ignorance which prevails.

Roth would allow competition on rural roads to overcome the dangers of monopoly. Fair enough, but one would not expect this to provide much of a safeguard. The barriers to entry are formidable. Capital costs are very high and the mere existence of monopoly profits will not be sufficient to bring the establishment of new roads. The potential road-owner will not calculate his returns on this capital on the basis of the monopoly prices but on the basis of the price that he will be able to charge, i.e. after competition has been introduced. This is likely to be very much lower, and if it is not, then the consumer will not have benefited (at least on price) in the way Roth expects. And if potential competition becomes actual, the possibilities of waste of scarce resources in running parallel and competing road networks are considerable.

And finally, the paternalist can and (I will assert) should fall back on his value-judgements. If it is consistent with his values, his idea of what is the good and humane society, that the old and the sick should be cared for free of direct charge to them and that there should be free and uniform education to give equality of opportunity, then there is no room for argument. As Richard Goode put it at the 1966 Conference of the Internation Institute of Public Finance, it is all very well for liberals to show that it is more efficient to have a free market in medicine; but as one travels around the world one keeps coming up against the fact that state provision for universal medical treatment is the will of the majority. If that is so then no amount of economic theory will count.

9 The Ability-to-Pay Approach

In so far as the benefit rule with its earmarked taxes and commercialized government services is rejected, we can turn to the second of the two traditional approaches to taxation. The ability-to-pay approach would abandon the attempt to get simultaneous determination of government expenditure and individual tax shares and would treat expenditure and revenue as two quite separate problems: the government would decide what its expenditure was to be in any one year, and this would determine what the appropriate amount of revenue would be. This *required yield* would be raised by taxing people, not according to how much they benefit from government expenditure, but according to their capacity to pay taxes – their ability-to-pay.

The measurement of ability

The first issue we have to discuss is what base to take for the measurement of ability to pay. The most obvious measure of ability to pay taxes, and the one most commonly used by governments, is income after allowances for subsistence – the subsistence allowance varying with family size and other circumstances. The greater one's money income the better able one is to pay taxes. It is clear that in a rational definition of income capital gains would be included. Gifts received and inheritances are other things which augment income but are often not regarded in such a light by the authorities.

But money income is not by any means the only or even the best measure of ability to pay. In the interests of horizontal equity, it would seem to be necessary to include allowances for non-money income. The income derived in the form of comfort or pleasure from the ownership of such things as houses, art treasures or jewellery, is no less real than the income derived from other types of investment. If one man invests £10,000 in equities and derives an income which is subject to taxation, then horizontal equity would require that another man who invested £10,000 in a picture because he preferred the kind of income derived from paintings should be similarly taxed. The 'Schedule A' tax which was abolished in Britain in 1962 was a proportional tax on the non-monetary income which was derived from the enjoyment of domestic property.

Ability to pay is also a function of wealth and wealth may be just as, or even more important than, income. It is possible to be very rich in assets with low yields, or with yields which are not of a monetary type. One may have one's assets in the form of antique furniture in stately country homes which yield no money income, and in the shares of companies which are growing so rapidly as to give negligible dividend yields. Indeed, there are companies whose policy it is to produce wealth but no income, profits all being re-invested in the growth of the company. These assets may produce little income but certainly enhance their proprietor's ability to pay taxes; they can be sold off in order to make tax payments. At the very least, assets reduce their owner's need to set aside something out of current income against misfortunes such as illness or for retirement.

But one's ability to pay taxes is not just a function of one's current flow of income or current stock of assets like government securities, bank accounts or property. Intangible assets and indeed liabilities may be just as important. Current ability to pay taxes is vitally affected by the expected future ability to earn income. A really satisfactory definition of wealth would include allowances for likely future income appropriately discounted to give its present value. Here we are considering mental and physical ability, health, age, training, and all the other determinants of future income. Indeed, the most satisfactory basis for assessing ability to pay taxes may be 'net worth'.

Net worth $= f(Y, A, Y_e)$, where Y is current income, A is net tangible assets and Y_e is net value of the expected future income stream discounted at the appropriate rate of interest to give its present value. The concept of net worth corresponds closely to the 'normal income' of the post-Keynesian consumption-function theories.

The importance of bringing expected future earnings into the calculation of ability to pay may be illustrated by reference to two individuals with identical salaries and asset holdings, one with twenty years to go before he retires while the other is serving his last year in employment. Other things being equal, the man whose income from employment is about to cease is clearly less able to pay taxes. The younger man has still got twenty years in which to build up his assets for use in his retirement.

Equity and ability to pay

The rationale of the ability-to-pay approach is that the payment of taxes involves the individual in a loss of utility – a sacrifice. The greater the ability to pay, the smaller the sacrifice involved in the payment of a unit of taxation. A fair system of taxation based on the ability-to-pay approach is defined as one where the sacrifices of utility by all taxpayers are equal. Vertical equity is served if all taxpayers bear an equal subjective burden of taxation. It is important to stress the word subjective. As we shall see, this does not imply that all taxpayers pay the same amount of money in taxes.

We now take a closer look at the concept of equal sacrifice in *order to define more clearly* exactly what is meant by 'equal' sacrifice and then proceed to examine what sort of tax regime would be commended by such an approach.

Three definitions of equality of sacrifice

From the discussion of taxation by ability to pay three possible interpretations of equal sacrifice have emerged. These are:

1. Equal absolute or equal total sacrifice.

2. Equal proportional sacrifice.

3. Equal marginal or least aggregate sacrifice.

Precisely what is meant by each of these three concepts and the choice (on cardinal welfare grounds) between them has been neatly demonstrated by Musgrave (1959).

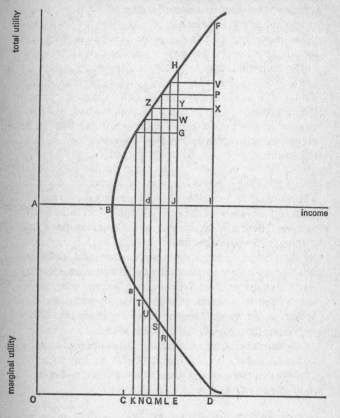

Figure 28

The assumptions of this model are:

1. The marginal utility of income declines as income rises.

2. One marginal utility of income schedule can be drawn to represent the utilities of all individuals in the economy. This

makes interpersonal utility comparisons (which are ruled out in the New Welfare Economics) possible.

3. Income has no meaningful utility below subsistence level. In Figure 28 subsistence is represented by AB.

4. The government has a given revenue requirement. This is the pre-Keynesian assumption of *required yield*. The required yield is represented in Figure 28 by CD.

5. Pre-tax incomes are given; they are not affected by the choice of distribution of tax burden, i.e. there are no dis-incentive effects.

Figure 28 shows the utility schedules which are common to two individuals; a rich man with pre-tax income OD and a poor man with pre-tax income OE. Their joint marginal utility schedule slopes downwards above the subsistence income level AB and their total utility schedule rises after income AB. Thus the total utility of the rich man's pre-tax income is FI units of utility and that of the poor man is HJ. The government requires a yield of CD from the combined payments of the two taxpayers.

Equal absolute sacrifice requires that both rich and poor men give up the same quantity of utility in such a way that their combined contributions (which must be unequal in terms of money payments) are equal to the required yield CD. The rich man pays LD in taxes and the poor man pays KE in taxes, so that LD + KE = CD. Although LD is greater than KE the two taxpayers have sacrificed the same amount of total utility, i.e. HG = FV. The rich man has paid more money in taxes than the poor man but both have found it equally unpleasant.

Note. So long as the marginal utility of income falls as income rises, equal absolute sacrifice will involve the rich in being taxed more heavily than the poor. How much more depends on the slope of the marginal utility schedules: the steeper the MUY schedule the more progressive the tax regime indicated. In fact a unit elastic MUY schedule suggests proportional taxation. If the elasticity of the MUY schedule is less than unity, regressive taxes are indicated and if the elasticity is more than unity, progressive taxes are indicated.

The *equal proportional sacrifice approach* suggests that a fair system of taxing according to ability to pay involves the rich not only in paying more money in taxes but in losing a greater absolute amount of utility: each gives up the same proportion of his utility in such a way that, in Figure 28, their combined contributions are equal to CD. Thus the rich man pays MD in taxes and the poor man pays NE, where NE + MD = CD. Although MD is greater than NE, each has given up the same proportion of the utility which he derived from his income. The rich man has given up PF of his total utility IF, and the poor man has given up WH of his total utility JH, where PF/IF = WH/JH.

Note. As with equal absolute sacrifice, the tax regime suggested by this concept of equal sacrifice will involve the rich in paying more than the poor as long as M U Y declines as income rises. Again the extent of progression (or otherwise) suggested varies with the slope of the M U Y schedule. If the utility of income is constant then proportional taxation is required. If the marginal utility declines more quickly than the average utility then progressive taxation is indicated. If the marginal utility of income declines more slowly than the average utility then regressive taxation is commended by the principle of equal proportional sacrifice.

The *equal marginal sacrifice approach* suggests that the rich man in our example should not only pay a greater amount in taxes but should sacrifice a *greater* proportion of his utility than the poor man. Each should pay taxes in such a way that the last unit of tax paid by each involves him in the same loss of utility as the other. Or to put it the other way round, the marginal utility of after-tax income should be the same for each individual. Again, combined tax payments must equal the required yield, CD. In Figure 28, the rich man pays QD in taxes and the poor man pays QE, where QE + QD = CD. The marginal sacrifice of rich and poor is equal at QU. The total sacrifice of the rich man is FX and the poor man's sacrifice is HY. The after-tax total utility of both tax-payers is the same at Zd = YJ = XI. In other words, what is being recommended by the equal marginal sacrifice rule is a regime which raises revenues by levelling down incomes so that after tax everyone has the same income. CD in revenue is raised by levelling both men's incomes down to OQ after tax. This is the complete egalitarian distribution of after-tax income.

Which equality of sacrifice?

We have then three possible interpretations of what is meant by equal sacrifice: equal absolute, equal proportional and equal marginal sacrifice. The question now arises: How do we choose between these three interpretations?

Two approaches are possible. The first is to ask which of these equalities of sacrifice is fairest? Which appeals to us most as fulfilling the requirement of vertical equity? Which provides the most appropriate or acceptable degree of inequality of taxation of people of different incomes? The answers to this question will be highly subjective and there may be considerable disagreement as to which is fairest. If 'generally acceptable' is the criterion of fairness which we adopt, then we have an important job for Gallup. My guess is that if the issue could be explained to the questionees, equal absolute or equal proportional sacrifice would command considerable support but that equal marginal sacrifice – implying the equalization of all post-tax incomes – would seem unfair to most.

The second approach is to ask which tax regime will produce the happiest community. This is possible in the cardinal utility model which we have been discussing and which is illustrated in Figure 28. Here it is possible to measure the total utility of this two-man community: total utility is equal to the rich man's total utility of income plus the poor man's total utility. One way of choosing between the three equity principles is to see which will give the greatest aggregate utility of income after tax when adding both men's total utilities.

We can find out which regime gives the highest total utility by reference to the bottom half of Figure 28, which shows the marginal utility of the income of both the rich and the poor man. Consider the after-tax marginal utilities of income of the two men under a regime of equal absolute sacrifice. The rich man's marginal utility of income is LR and the poor man's marginal utility of income is Ka. Clearly Ka is greater than LR; a dollar more or less means more to the poor man than to the rich man. This being the case, it is clear that the total utility of this community is not being maximized. It could be improved by increasing the rich man's tax burden by one unit and decreasing the poor man's burden by one unit. This will increase total utility by Ka — LR. The marginal utilities of the two men will still be unequal after such a re-allocation, so that further improvements are possible.

Re-allocation of income units from the rich man to the poor man for whom they have a higher utility can be pursued until the point is reached where the two taxpayers are making equal proportional sacrifice – the second interpretation of equal sacrifice. This position has been reached by making a series of improvements on the distribution of post-tax income obtaining under equal absolute sacrifice. So we can say that, on cardinal welfare grounds, equal proportional sacrifice is a better principle than equal absolute sacrifice: equal proportional sacrifice gives a greater total utility to the community. The marginal utility of income of the rich man is now SM and that of the poor man TN.

But notice that SM is smaller than TN. Equal proportional sacrifice also gives a sub-optimal distribution of income. Total utility is not being maximized. It is possible to increase the total utility of the community by taking another unit of income from the rich man and giving it to the poor man. This will increase the community's total utility by TN — SM. In fact, it should be clear that improvements in the total utility of a community will be possible so long as the marginal utilities of income of its members are not equal. In other words, it is only when the principle of equal marginal sacrifice is employed that no re-allocation of the tax burden will be capable of producing an increase in the total utility of the community.

Equal marginal sacrifice, then, emerges as the best principle on the grounds of minimizing the total burden of taxation. It may alternatively be called the principle of least aggregate sacrifice. This reasoning led Pigou to the conclusion that equal marginal sacrifice was the only acceptable rule on welfare grounds. And clearly, within the context of the model we have used, it is so.

Some objections to the sacrifice approach

Before we rush off and advocate an egalitarian distribution of after-tax income, we must recognize a long and imposing list of objections to the model which we have used. The explicit and implicit assumptions of the model vary from the questionable to the quite unacceptable:

1. The first assumption which we must query is the assumption of required yield; the assumption that the government seeks to raise a given amount of revenue (CD in Figure 28). The equal marginal sacrifice principle is the logical extension of the view that a pound's worth of the tax levied on the rich gives rise to less disutility than a similar tax levied on the poor. In Figure 29 ABCD is smaller than EFGH, where OA is a rich man's income and OE a poor man's income. This is intuitively plausible even if neither of assumptions 1 or 2 on page 134 is accepted. But what of the economic efficiency of taxes? The government is not, in the post-Keynesian era, interested primarily in a pound's worth of extra revenue. What it is interested in is a pound's worth of reduced private expenditure. Can we say with equal certainty that *a pound's worth of deflation* achieved by taxing the rich will cause less loss of utility than *a pound's worth of deflation* achieved by taxing the poor? We shall call 'a pounds worth of deflation' 'a unit of absorption'.

To facilitate the study of the significance of economic efficiency for the sacrifice approach, we make a simplification that investment is determined by expectations and the rate of interest which are both determined exogenously. Then only consumption expenditure is affected by taxation. What we have to consider here is the effects upon the consumption of various

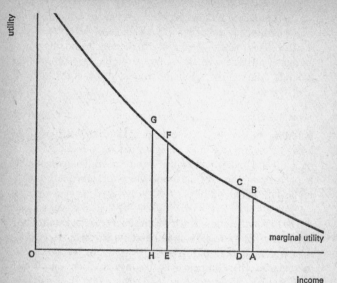

Figure 29

income groups of changes in taxes. If the rich and the poor have the same marginal propensities to consume, then the assumption of required yield will hold. The authorities will require a given revenue irrespective of who pays the tax. But it is almost certain that the marginal propensity to consume declines as income rises. A rich man who faces a tax increase will cut his consumption by less than a poor man faced with a similar tax increase. Therefore to bring about a given reduction in consumption the government will have to tax the rich man more heavily than the poor man. There is not a straight choice between raising £x from the poor or £x from the rich. Indeed, if one unit of absorption is required and can be achieved by a tax of £x on the poor man, a tax of £x on the rich man will fail to absorb enough private expenditure and prices will rise and both taxpayers will suffer a decline in real income. The government must choose between taking £x from the poor or £(x + n) from the rich. The ratio x/(x + n) is ascertained by a

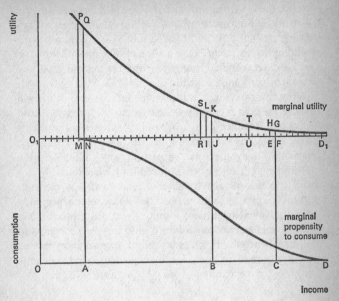

Figure 30

consideration of the marginal propensity to consume of the individual taxpayers.

In Figure 30, the top half of the diagram shows the utility of income schedule which is common to all taxpayers. The bottom half shows the marginal propensity to consume schedule which is also assumed to be common to all consumer-taxpayers. The marginal utility of income declines as income rises but additional income is assumed always to have some utility, however large income gets. The marginal propensity to consume is assumed to be unity for poor people. But as income rises, more and more of marginal income is saved until near the top of the income scale the marginal propensity to consume of the Kennedys, Rockefellers and Gettys is zero. There is some empirical evidence to suggest that the marginal propensity to consume of the individual is not unlike that depicted in Figure 30. By definition people at or below subsistence spend all their incomes and, in 1960, Getty reportedly spent $30,000 throwing a party for a thousand guests. Even during that party he was earning money faster than he was spending it. In circumstances of such extreme wealth it is unlikely that marginal changes in after-tax income make any impact on consumption at all.

Now if we wish to consider which income tax regime will impose the least sacrifice on taxpayers as a whole, we should not consider the sacrifices involved in making equal payments to the exchequer as we have so far. If we want to discuss in a meaningful way the least unpleasant way of fulfilling the government's fiscal objective of reducing expenditure by the private sector, we must consider unequal money payments to the government by rich and poor. The extent of the inequality of tax payment to achieve a unit of reduced expenditure is ascertained from a consideration of the marginal propensity to consume schedule. In order to reduce consumption by one unit it is necessary to tax an individual one unit times the reciprocal of the marginal propensity to consume.

$$R = \frac{C}{\text{MPC}}$$

where R is the revenue required, C is the reduction in consumption required, and MPC is the marginal propensity to consume.

In Figure 30, the axis O_1D_1 is marked off with two scales. Above O_1D_1 is marked a scale of units of revenue or income. From this it is possible to ascertain the sacrifices involved by different tax-payers in the payments of equal units of taxation. Below O_1D_1 is marked a scale of units of revenue required in order to reduce consumption by one unit. We shall call these units, units of absorption.

Let us assume that there are three taxpayer–consumers whose after-tax incomes are OA, OB and OC. The marginal propensity of the poorest (income OA) is one. The marginal propensity to consume of the middle income taxpayer (OB) is a half, and the marginal propensity to consume of the richest (OC) is one-eighth. Now suppose that the government wishes to make a marginal increase in taxation. If the authorities were simply after an increase in the revenue in increasing taxes, the least-sacrifice way of raising an extra unit of revenue is clearly to tax the rich man because his marginal sacrifice EFGH is smaller than the middle man's income marginal sacrifice IJKL which is smaller than the poor man's sacrifice MNQP.

But what if, as we know to be the usual case, the authorities want not an increment of revenue but an incremental decrease in the level of consumption? What if they want to change taxation by one unit of absorption? This entails raising one unit of revenue from the poor man or two units from the middle-income man or eight units of revenue from the rich man. In which case it is no longer certain that a government which wishes to minimize the sacrifices involved in paying its taxes will, even given the assumptions of this model, increase the taxation of the rich.

In Figure 30 we see that the sacrifice of the poor man in giving up one unit of absorption will be MNQP. The middle-income man will suffer a loss of satisfaction equal to RJKS in paying two units of tax. And the rich man will suffer a loss of utility equal to UFGT while taxation reduces his income by eight units. In fact in Figure 30, these sacrifices appear to be about equal. This has no general significance, of course, and the result depends upon the slopes of the M U Y schedule and the M P C schedules. The steeper the slope of the M U Y schedule and the less steep the M P C schedule, the stronger the case for taxing the rich on welfare grounds. If the M U Y schedule declines slowly enough and the M P C declines quickly enough, the case may be made *on cardinal welfare grounds* for taxing the poor and exempting the rich altogether, not that this is ever likely to be made as a serious policy suggestion. Verification awaits empirical evidence which in the case of the marginal utility of income is hardly likely to be forthcoming.

If *economic efficiency* is important the assumption of required yield is misleading. The equal sacrifice approach (Figure 28) is not comparing like with like in considering the taxation of rich and poor. In order to get a meaningful picture the tax contribution of each individual must be weighted to take account of his marginal propensity to spend.

2. Students of the new welfare economics will know that it is held that the cardinal welfare approach, whereby it is deemed possible in principle to measure utility, and to add one man's utility to another man's and compare the utilities of several men, is inadmissible. In the new welfare economics *interpersonal utility comparisons* are out.

Though we can accept the assumption that each individual at any instant in time will have a declining marginal utility of income schedule, the assumption that all individuals in the economy share the same marginal utility schedule is quite unacceptable. This implies that all individuals have the same tastes and preferences. This is obviously not the case. It would be easy, for example, to find two people who had equal incomes, one of whom had little desire for more money, feeling that he had sufficient income to meet his needs, while the other was desperately short of money and willing to go to great lengths to earn more. Clearly these two people have very different marginal utilities of income.

Similarly, while we may accept the general proposition that on the whole a marginal pound is worth more to a poor man than to a rich man, it is unrealistic to assume that people of different incomes will share the same marginal utility of income schedule. There can be little doubt, for example, that as people grow richer they acquire new tastes and I would be prepared to guess that the marginal utility schedule moves up with income.

3. The static nature of this model makes policy conclusions more difficult. The implicit assumption – that the pre-tax income of both rich and poor man is given and will be unaffected by the tax regime employed – is all right for a static model but will not bear generalization to a dynamic real world. If the rich man finds that of his pre-tax income OD all that above OQ is taken in taxation, will he not act 'rationally' and take things a bit easier, so that his pre-tax income falls to OQ which will

leave his post-tax income the same? In a two-person economy this is unlikely to happen, because any reduction in the rich man's contribution to the exchequer arising out of his reduced pre-tax income will have to be made up by increasing the tax rates equally on both men (if the equal marginal principle is to be maintained). But where are the two-person economies? In the real world there will be so many people in any economy that no action of one individual in reducing his share of tax payments will materially affect the level above which the government lops off all incomes (OQ). A 'rational' man will reduce his work effort and his pre-tax income. So will all tax-payers; and national income will fall because the 'incentive' to work is removed.

Perhaps when national income has fallen, the 'rational' actions may turn out to have been irrational. And perhaps we should describe the way people act in a market economy as 'selfish' rather than 'rational'. Individual producers and consumers pursue their own selfish ends, and guided by the 'invisible hand' which controls markets they incidentally pursue ends which benefit society as a whole. This is how Adam Smith described the relationship between the pursuit of private gain and the attainment of general welfare in the capitalist system. And it is true today that capitalism still operates by giving people incentives in the form of higher after-tax income, so that they will work harder to earn bigger bonuses, bigger profits or promotion. It seems very likely that the selfish pursuit of greater income after tax is an important factor in the promotion of economic growth.

But what is suggested as a tax policy by our static cardinal utility model is that all income differentials be removed by taxation. This is likely to reduce the size of the National Income to be divided among the people in the future. And though after-tax equality can be shown to maximize total utility in the short run, it seems likely that it would reduce total utility over time.

Marx, of course, believed that after various selfish tensions in people had been removed by years of socialist life, incentives would become unnecessary and a communist society could thrive with an egalitarian distribution. While one may hope that, at some future time, selfishness will disappear as an important motive force in society, clearly Western society meanwhile has to live with capitalism for which the incentive afforded by post-tax income differentials is essential.

In short, the model depicted in Figure 28 is not capable of providing important policy conclusions, because it ignores the likely consequences of tax policy upon future income.

Summary

What we have done here is to give rigorous expression to the very widespread belief that the rich should pay more in taxes than the poor and indeed that there should be progressive taxation – that the rich should pay a larger proportion of their incomes in taxes, because the payment of taxes hurts the rich less. We have pursued this view to its logical extremity but found that the model necessary to do so was wanting in several respects. Before we can define an optimal policy for the distribution of after-tax income we will have to measure utility, measure propensities to consume, and quantify the relationship between incentives and growth. We will then need a social time-preference rate to facilitate the choice between present and future income.

The cardinal approach to equity in taxation has not taken us very far. But although the type of universal income utility relationship depicted in Figure 28 is clearly an oversimplification, the proposition that interpersonal comparisons of utility have no scientific validity is not everywhere accepted. While we need not go as far as Georgescu-Roegen (1954, 1966) or Harsanyi (1955) many will accept that there is at least a two-tier hierarchy of wants – basic necessities up to subsistence and other wants and, secondly, that interpersonal comparisons could be made – even at the margin – between people seeking to satisfy basic wants and those seeking to satisfy lower-order wants.

In any case as Simon (1938) observed that 'the case for equality is enormously stronger than any utility foundation on which it can be rested'. The ability-to-pay approach to taxation can be justified in terms of benefits indirectly bestowed on the rich by the imposed social milieu or increased stability of society or in terms of the moral unacceptability of extreme income differentials. If the welfare of the rich is a positive function of the welfare of the poor, then the benefit and ability-to-pay approaches tend to coalesce.

10 The Income-Maximization Approach

The government may, and to varying extents always does, design its tax strategy with the objective of producing a higher national income than would obtain in the absence of government intervention. The income-maximization approach to taxation, which has gained great impetus from the post-war interest in growth, would choose that regime which produced the greatest national income. Thus taxes and negative taxes (subsidies) are used so to intervene in the market as to induce a greater output of goods and services.

Tax–subsidy policy can influence the size of the National Income in two ways. Firstly, by inducing a series of once-and-for-all adjustments in the allocation of scarce resources in the economy so as to produce a bigger income from given resources. This is the static approach. Secondly, the dynamic approach to income maximization through taxation, is that which seeks to promote the acceleration of growth from year to year of national income. This is attempted by identifying those factors which are growth-promoting and subsidizing them or making profits accruing from them subject to tax relief, and by identifying those factors which are growth inhibiting and making them subject to penal taxation.

Once-and-for-all income increasing measures

Tax/subsidy policy for increasing/decreasing cost firms

In a perfectly competitive economy, the country's scarce resources will be used optimally in as much as each firm will be operating at the point of minimum average cost. But, of course, no one lives in a perfectly competitive market and all manner of market imperfections do exist. Monopolists, who restrict output to raise price, will only operate at the point of minimum average cost by accident, and the size of the firm in relation to the size of the market for particular products may mean that a wide range of positions on their average cost curves are taken by firms.

Marshall (1890) first pointed out the possibility of increasing the efficiency of utilization of country's scarce resources, and so of the real national income, by taxing firms which were over-producing and subsidizing firms which were underproducing. Given a U-shaped average cost curve, this meant taxing firms operating under conditions of increasing average costs and subsidizing those which were operating in conditions of declining average costs. Pigou (1929) came to the same conclusions but we shall illustrate the point in Marshallian terms.

Figure 31 (a) shows the demand and cost situation facing a firm operating in conditions of falling average cost. The firm is operating on an average cost (plus a normal profit) basis, selling output OQ_1 for a price of OP_1 per unit. This output is clearly sub-optimal, because at output OQ_1 there are still people who want to buy the good in question and are willing to pay more than the marginal cost of producing extra units. A subsidy which lowered average cost to AC_1 would lead to the production of some of these units. This would lead to a movement down the AC schedule and the gross-of-subsidy average

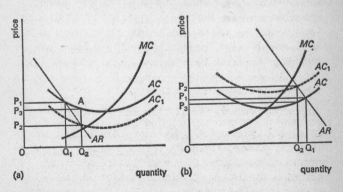

Figure 31

cost would be lowered to Q_2A by moving towards the point of minimum average cost.

Price is lowered by more than the subisdy $P_2P_1 > P_2P_3$.

Figure 31 (b) shows the demand and costs facing a firm operating in conditions of rising average cost. That is to say, marginal cost is above average cost and units of output are being produced, the marginal cost of which is greater than what consumers would be willing to pay. Output is extended beyond the point of least average cost. AC_1 shows what happens to average cost if a tax is placed on the good concerned. Price rises to OP_2 and the quantity produced falls to OQ_2. This tax has the converse beneficial effect to the subsidy represented in Figure 31 (a). Average cost (net of tax this time) again falls as output is reduced towards the point of minimum average cost, and output $Q_1 Q_2$ (for which consumers were not willing to pay the marginal cost) is no longer produced.

Price is raised by less than the tax; $P_2P_1 < P_2P_3$.

Thus a tax levied on increasing-cost industries the proceeds of which are used to subsidize the output of decreasing-cost industries will have a beneficial effect on real income. As resources are moved from the production of one good to the production of the other, both goods are produced more efficiently in the sense that both will be produced at a lower cost of scarce resources – at a lower point in the average cost (net of tax, gross of subsidy) schedule. And this output, which uses resources more efficiently, more accurately reflects consumer preferences. Resources which were producing goods for which the consumers were not willing to pay the marginal cost are diverted to producing goods the marginal costs of which the consumers were willing to pay but which were not being produced.

This conclusion is straightforward enough but it is not so simple when one comes to applying this sort of argument as economic policy. Apart from the theoretical arguments there is the question of clear identification and accurate measurement of the cost schedules involved. And, most importantly, the distinction between long-run and short-run costs. There are also the questions of what sort of taxation and what sort of subsidy are to be employed in order to shake resources out of rising cost into declining cost industries, and how flexible the resources in question are. When the British government announced its intention to shift resources from services to manufactures in 1966, a British businessman made the point about resource flexibility with heavy sarcasm when he said, 'My works manager is crying out for two shot-firers and a fitter. He will be delighted when I tell him that the government is going to provide him with a barber and two croupiers'. Of course, no one intended that anybody change from a croupier to a skilled engineer. It was anticipated that a series of short steps involving many people and leaving an all round decrease in service employment would take place. Nevertheless, as we shall see on pages 53–5, there are cases where resource flexibility may be low.

And a falling average cost in one industry and rising average costs in another is not a sufficient condition for a tax/subsidy policy. The government will have to take into account external costs and benefits of production and consumption of the goods in question before deciding to act. It is only when average social costs have been added to those of the private average costs that a government will have a basis for action on the grounds that firms are selling at above or below marginal cost.

Despite these difficulties, however, there are cases where the logic of this argument is taken into account by governments. The British decision to support the domestic computer industry, taken in 1964, was based on the observation that this industry was one in which overheads were very high and where variable costs were less important: the industry faced a steeply downward sloping average cost curve. The government's decisions to subsidize the industry by placing large orders with it was done partly in the knowledge that this large order would allow the industry considerably to spread overheads and so reduce prices.

The policy of marginal cost pricing of public utilities, which is dealt with by Turvey (1968), would lead to other situations in which increasing cost industries would be taxed to subsidize decreasing-cost industries. The average cost of using a bridge or a tunnel clearly falls the more it is used, since the marginal cost of using such a utility after it is built may be assumed to be negligible (ignoring, for the moment, possible congestion costs). Any price at all for this bridge or tunnel would be above marginal cost and would therefore cause some people who would have liked to use the bridge at a lower or zero price to be deterred from using it. This implies an under-utilization of the bridge – a less than maximal flow of real income or consumers surplus from this investment. For this reason it is often decided to build public utilities out of public funds and to allow their use at the zero price.

It is at most a short step from the increasing–decreasing cost discussion to the other set of once-for-all income increasing tax/subsidy measures which governments take.

Redistributing demand between products

When an economy is suffering from a scarcity of resources in relation to the demands which are being made upon them at a given price level (when there is inflation), the inflationary pressure will not be felt evenly throughout the economy. There will, even in the most inflationary times when most firms are working at full capacity and average costs are starting to rise, be some firms or industries or some regions, which are suffering from insufficient demand; where factories are working at below capacity and so face downward sloping average costs.

The government can achieve an increase in real national income by diverting demand from those industries which are working at full capacity (where the industry is experiencing rising prices or queueing) to those industries which have idle capacity and where an increase in output will lead to the spreading of fixed costs over a greater output. Taxation of the prosperous industries and/or subsidization of those with excess capacity may allow a greater output to be produced while keeping prices down.

However, this is not a policy which could be pursued at all times without cost. One must ask why it is that some industries are experiencing expansion which is too rapid for them to cope with, while others cannot sell all of their potential output. The answer is likely to be that tastes and preferences of consumers are altering in such a way that the output of the depressed industry is subject to a secular decline and that the industries which are fully employed are fully employed because they produce the goods of the present and future. In this case, what is required is the movement of scarce resources out of the obsolete industries into the new ones. This would normally be brought about by high profits in the new industries and bankruptcies in the declining industries. Any government action to subsidize the declining industries and tax the growing industries will have the effect of retarding these changes. In other words, this action may produce a bigger national income but one of lower quality in the sense that it reflects less accurately consumer's choices. Extensive efforts to ensure that all the nation's productive capacity is always in use through tax/subsidy policies are capable of producing a situation where prices reflect costs so inaccurately, that national income statistics become meaningless because one cannot know if or to what extent output mirrors consumers' choices.

Nevertheless, there are situations in which governments apply this static income-maximizing tax/subsidy strategem, and indeed quite a strong case for so doing can be made under certain circumstances.

The thing which determines the appropriateness of such measures is the *flexibility* of the resources in question. How long and at what sort of cost will it take to get the land, labour and capital out of the declining industries into those which are short of men and materials? If the resources are absolutely flexible and can be transferred in a day, then any propping up of declining industries will indeed inhibit the development of the new. If, on the other hand, the machinery is non-flexible and the labour is too old or too ignorant to learn new skills at any cost, then the alternatives to tax-subsidy policy to spread demand evenly will be inflation in growth sectors and waste in the declining sectors. It is better to have the resources in the declining sectors producing something, even if it is not exactly what consumers want, rather than producing nothing.

The extremes of flexibility or non-flexibility are not likely to occur. Real-world situations will be cases of greater or less flexibility. All we can say is the lower the resource flexibility, the more appropriate becomes the policy of redistributing demand from over-employed to under-employed industry.

Two examples from British experience will serve as illustration:

1. The British coal industry is subject to rapidly diminishing labour employment because of a slow secular decline in the demand for coal accompanied by a rapid rise in labour productivity. This combination of circumstances has necessitated a policy of closing down many loss-making pits. The absorption of this steady stream of ex-miners by the labour market takes place with greatest ease in periods of high and rising employment. The miners' skill tends to be inflexible so that periods of retraining have to be undertaken. The higher the unemployment level, the more likely retraining is to be necessary.

In the winter of 1966, unemployment in Britain was rising rapidly and was expected to go a good deal higher. In this case many miners who became redundant would have had to undergo extensive retraining or suffer a period of unemployment. Retraining facilities being very limited, closing pits in this period, although it would save the National Coal Board some money, would not provide any real savings. It was thought better from the point of view of maximizing National Income to have the men producing some coal (even at a loss) rather than being idle. For this reason some projected pit closures were postponed until spring when re-employment prospects normally improve with the seasonal rise in employment.

2. In the early 1960s the British shipbuilding industry was suffering from a shortage of orders, excess capacity, poor or negative returns on capital and shrinking employment. Many of the shipbuilding skills were highly flexible which made much of the labour employed in the yards attractive to other sectors of the engineering industry. However, the capital equipment employed in shipbuilding was highly inflexible,

being of little more than scrap value in the case of closure of yards.

The government took certain steps in 1965 to subsidize this industry on the grounds that this would benefit the National Income. Normally one would say that the best course of action would be to transfer resources from this declining sector of the economy to one which was growing, and that to prop up the declining industries would reduce GNP by inhibiting the growth of the new industries. But this is only true if it is believed that the decline is permanent. And the British Government had just received the report of the Geddes Committee (1966) which forecast a boom in shipbuilding in the near future. If the closure of yards had gone on unchecked, Britain would have been caught short of shipbuilding capacity and so much inflexible capital equipment would have been wastefully scrapped.

The Geddes Committee forecast has proved substantially correct and British shipyards were by 1968 fully employed. It is still very much open to question whether subsidization of the yards was fruitful as some were still showing poor or negative returns on capital employed, but it does illustrate the proposition that governments may attempt to increase income by redistributing demand from over-employed resources to under employed resources.

Redistributing demand between regions

The other and (quantitatively) most important attempt to produce a greater income by using existing resources more fully is dealt with under the heading of *regional policy*. In all capitalist economies there are substantial variations in the employment ratios from region to region. Some regions have unemployment rates several times higher than the national average and this seems to be a permanent feature of most depressed regions. Unemployment represents wasted resources of labour. The existence of unemployment means a smaller National Income than could have been achieved with full employment.

Since Keynesian Public Finance came to be understood and accepted, the danger of mass and general unemployment has been eliminated by budget deficits and appropriate monetary policy. But as soon as *some regions* reach full employment, shortages appear and inflation becomes a problem. Meanwhile other regions will still be far from fully employed and there is nothing that can be done by Keynesian full-employment policies further to augment employment. What is required to get the idle capacity in depressed regions into employment is not an increase in effective demand but a redistribution of effective demand from the fully-employed to the under-employed areas by tax–subsidy policy. By eliminating such pockets of unemployment the authorities aim to increase income. This formed an important plank in the British Government's Economic Plan of 1965. It was proposed to augment the labour force by bringing the pockets of unemployment into fuller employment.

It should be recognized that, as with the previous cases, regional employment policy, while increasing income in the short term, may not do so in the longer term. Depressed regions may be depressed because there is some inherent disadvantage associated with economic activity there. It may be that the best policy for growth in the long run would be to allow the invisible hand of the market-place to guide resources towards those parts of the country which are best suited to economic development.

However, there are areas where, because labour mobility is so low, the alternative to regional tax–subsidy policy is chronic unemployment and wasted resources of labour. There may also be circumstances in which a case may be made for reversing what is seen to be the natural movement of resources towards the prosperous concentrations of population. In the case of the drift to the south-east of England, for example, the British government takes the view that allowing this to go on unabated is not consistent with maximizing national income because of the divergence of private and social costs – those people who flock into the south-east consider only private costs and benefits. They don't consider the congestion costs they impose on others, and the extensive social overhead capital that is provided largely by the national exchequer, for their needs. We have been talking, as best befits economists, about quantitative increases in National Income. We must observe, however, that an important argument in the political economy of regional development is the qualitative argument that a society in which the population is more evenly spread provides a higher form of life to a concentrated one, and that in any case Western economies are rich enough to afford a little subsidization of economic backwaters in the interests of equity.

Fiscal reflation

The most spectacular gains in income resulting from government intervention are to be had when unemployed resources exist throughout the economy. If the productive potential of the economy has been rising more rapidly than output, there will be a margin of unused productive capacity in the economy and unemployed labour. In these circumstances, which existed in Britain in 1958–9 and in the United States in 1962–3, a dramatic increase in income may be achieved by government policies (monetary, fiscal or both) to increase demand. Fiscal reflation involves altering the balance of deflationary taxes and inflationary government expenditures. Taxes will normally be reduced while expenditure is allowed to rise. This pump-priming will be reinforced by multipler and accelerator effects which raise effective demand. When increased demand appears, businessmen will put their idle capacity and men to work to satisfy the augmented demand.

In Britain in 1959 taxes were cut and government expenditure allowed to increase. Demand rose and unemployment fell until in 1961 output had caught up with productive potential. Then inflation set in and real growth slowed down. But for more than two years Britain enjoyed a doubling of the trend growth rate. In the United States, though the pump was first primed by relaxation of monetary policy, fiscal reflation, under the Kennedy Administration, played a notable part in the accelerated growth which lasted until perhaps 1967 when unemployment reached historically low levels and output had caught up with productive capacity.

It must be understood that fiscal reflation cannot take the credit for all of the output gains in these periods of rapid growth. If the underlying growth of productive potential is 3 per cent and opportunities for fiscal reflation arise and are taken, raising growth to 5 per cent, then this measure has only contributed 2 per cent to the growth rate. And these gains are of a once-for-all nature. It is only by increasing the rate of growth of productive potential that cumulative increases in income can be achieved.

Measures designed to accelerate growth of income

The once-for-all increases in National Income which it is possible to promote by tax/subsidy policies and which were described in the previous section, though no doubt of some interest, are quantitatively insignificant, compared with the potential gains to a tax system which could accelerate the rate of growth. A 5 per cent gain in income as a result of the once for all measures would mean, at best, that income would be raised permanently by 5 per cent. But a tax measure or series of measures which could raise the British average rate of growth from 3 per cent to 5 per cent would mean that, because of compound interest effects, the national income in twenty years would be one-and-a-half times what it would otherwise have been, and in forty years the benefits of raising the growth rate would amount to a more than doubling of the real income. It can be seen that this section is potentially the most important in this book.

The acceleration of growth by tax–subsidy policy involves examining the process of economic growth, identifying those factors which are growth inhibiting and discouraging them by taxation, and identifying those factors which are growth promoting and encouraging these with subsidies.

Without going at all deeply into growth theory, it is fairly easy to identify many of the important factors inhibiting or promoting growth. A growth-conscious government would seek by its taxation policy to encourage saving, technological advance, investment, hard work and efficient use of resources by business management. They would seek to inhibit consumption and the wasteful use of scarce resources.

It will at once be objected that consumption is not growth inhibiting. It is widely believed (and rightly so) that a high level of consumption is in fact vital to a fast rate of growth. Businessmen are not going to invest in order to increase output unless they are confident that they will be able to sell that output. On the other hand, we know from our national income analysis that with any given income, investment and consumption are in fact alternatives: $Y = C + I$.

Consumption, then, must be high in order to encourage investment, but low so that resources are available for investment. This apparent paradox is explained with the aid of Figure 32. Here consumption and investment are plotted so that OD is the 100 per cent consumption of income schedule. C shows a high propensity to consume, and C_1 a low propensity to consume. OE is the full-employment income, and $C + I$ is the consumption function plus the investment function.

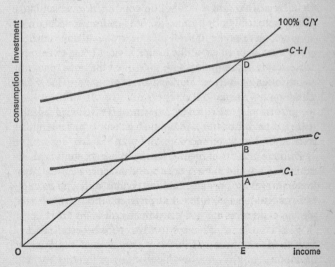

Figure 32

When we say we want consumption to be low, we mean that the consumption function should be as far to the right as possible. In other words, C_1 is preferred to C in the interests of growth. The lower consumption function allows AD of investment to take place at full employment, whereas the higher consumption function only allows for BD of investment out of the full employment income OE.

On the other hand, given the consumption function C_1, it is important that consumption be as high as EA, otherwise there will be deficient demand. The full-employment output will not be saleable, and investment and growth will fall.

So the paradox is resolved. The government tries to discourage consumption (encourage saving) out of any given income, but uses compensatory fiscal policy to ensure that the given income (and so consumption) is as high as can be produced in conditions of full employment.

Tax/subsidy policy for consumption and saving

Governments try to move the consumption function to the right by a wide range of taxes on consumption which make saving relatively more attractive. (Of course, reducing consumption in response to taxes may be irrational unless there is some hope than when, in the future, savings come to be spent tax rates on consumption have fallen.) At the same time, saving is often actively encouraged by a series of inducements based on tax exemption.

For example, in Britain income which is saved via life insurance is exempt from tax. And though income from investments as a whole are taxed more heavily than 'earned' income, in Britain the first £15 earned on savings bank accounts is allowed free of tax, and in both Britain and America taxation of increases in value of savings, i.e. capital gains, although certainly part of real income, is taxed at preferential rates. Moreover, capital gains taxes are not levied unless the gains are realized. This is a powerful incentive to save: people become locked into their investments in order to avoid gains tax liability.

Measures to stimulate investment

Arrow (1962) has pointed out that there are important external benefits accruing to society as a whole from investment. If private entrepreneurs invest, they will reap the direct benefits in increased output. But there will also be a 'technological fall-out' in increased knowledge and training which will increase output in industries other than those which made the original investment. Because total benefits exceed private benefits, investment will always be sub-optimal in a free private-enterprise economy. In order to achieve optimal investment government stimulation must be given.

We can distinguish three phases in the investment process: pure research; the application of knowledge gained from pure research to the development of new or better techniques of production; and the application of these proven techniques throughout industry as a whole. The external benefits of investment are likely to be most important in pure research, less important in development, and not so important in the case of applying proven techniques throughout industry. For this reason government subsidization of investment is concentrated particularly on the research and development sides.

Indeed, the external benefits of pure research predominate to such an extent as to raise serious doubts about how much would be done if there were no state support. And 77 per cent of British basic research and 63 per cent of the research in the USA is undertaken directly by the government or government-sponsored institutions. Also, the space programs and military programs from which there is an important external benefit in knowledge about metals, for example, clearly have the sort of payoff which is too uncertain to be undertaken by private enterprise.

There are also widespread inducements given by governments to encourage private enterprise to undertake more investment by reducing the cost of investment. These are of three main types: loans at lower interest rates than are available on the market, subsidies, and tax exemptions.

Favourable depreciation arrangements. A company buying a machine which is reckoned to last ten years will be able to count a tenth of the cost of the machine as an operating expense in each tax year of the life of the machine. Thus if the machine costs £100 then 10 per cent is written off in each year and profit reduced by £10. If corporation tax is 40 per cent, then the companies tax bill is reduced by £4 per year. Now this seems fair enough, but while it does mean that the real cost of the investment is not £100 but £60 (ignoring for the moment the cost to the firm involved in waiting for payment of the £40 over ten years), one would hesitate to describe depreciation under these arrangements as a subsidy to investment. If a corporation tax of 40 per cent reduces the cost of making an investment, so does it reduce the returns to that investment – by 40 per cent. But depreciation may be made more favourable so as to stimulate investment.

Provision may be made for depreciating over a shorter period our machine whose life span is ten years. *Accelerated depreciation* will mean that the tax relief is brought forward in time. British *Initial Allowances* would have allowed our firm to write off not 10 but 20 per cent of the investment in the first year and the rest over the next eight years. What this amounts to is bringing the £4 tax exemption forward from the tenth to the first year of operation. It is in fact a nine-year interest-free loan of £4. It has the advantage that it increases the companies' cash flow when it is most needed – when investments are being undertaken. Initial allowances can be much more generous than the above example, the ultimate concession being *free depreciation* which allows companies to write off capital expenditure at any rate they choose. The whole tax relief may then be taken in the first year if there are enough profits to relieve.

Another favourable treatment of investment expenditure has been provided in Britain under the heading of *investment allowances*. This operates in the same way as initial allowances except that although it is possible to write off as much as 40 per cent against tax in the first year, our firm would be allowed to write off 10 per cent not for the next six years, but for the next nine years. A total of £130 worth of tax allowances would have been received although the machine only cost £100. With a corporation tax of 40 per cent this represents a subsidy to this investment of £12 (12 per cent).

These favourable provisions for depreciation, which have been used also as instruments of the government's attempts to influence the regional distribution of industry, have been very disappointing in their impact. The currently fashionable explanation of this is that a large proportion of British managements make their investment decisions with pre-tax profits in mind. This extraordinary state of affairs means that any tax concessions are simply regarded as a pleasant bonus but do not influence investment decisions. This method of subsidy is felt to be too uncertain and involve too long a wait for reimbursement. For these reasons the British government changed in 1966 to a policy of direct subsidization of investment.

Subsidies for investment. Governments may try to increase the rate of investment by direct subsidies. In Britain all investment was subsidized; plant and machinery at up to 45 per cent and buildings at up to 35 per cent, depending mainly on the location of the investment. This had the effect of greatly increasing the returns on capital employed. A 40 per cent grant raises to 17 per cent the return on an investment which would have yielded 10 per cent. However, the government elected in 1970 decided to return to the investment allowance system, mainly because allowances encourage efficiency as only profitable firms can claim them.

Other tax measures to stimulate investment

In both Britain and the United States, a strong incentive to company savings and, so it is hoped, to investment by the companies, is given by the system of company taxation. Thus company profits are subjected to a corporation tax of $42\frac{1}{2}$ per cent in Britain and up to 60 per cent in the United States. That part of the company's profits which is passed on to shareholders in dividends is then taxed again at the marginal rate of tax appropriate to the shareholders in question. Now the whole of a company belongs to the shareholders and whether or not the profits are distributed to these shareholders, they do form a part of the shareholders' income. The shareholders have in effect a choice between leaving their profits with the company for reinvestment, in which case their company will be worth more, and taking their profits out of the company and paying much higher rates of tax. In Britain, retained profits are taxed at $42\frac{1}{2}$ per cent whereas distributed profits will be subjected to total income and corporation taxes of from $42\frac{1}{2}$ per cent to 92·95 per cent. This being the case, a strong incentive exists to leave profits within the company for reinvestment. Some companies have a declared policy of offering their shareholders a growing company and modestly taxed capital gains rather than highly taxed dividends.

There is little doubt that the double taxation of distributed profits provides a powerful incentive to company saving, and that this system of company taxation leads to a shift to the right of the consumption functions in Figure 32. However, as we shall see in the next section, it is open to question whether this is altogether good for growth.

Increasing the quality of investment

We have been suggesting that the government can, through the fiscal system, help accelerate growth in the national income by seeing that a greater proportion of the country's scarce resources are devoted to investment. But there is another important way in which fiscal policy can be used to enhance growth, and that is by encouraging the efficient use of any given amount of scarce resources. Market forces *tend* to encourage efficiency. The profitable ventures succeed, the harder working earn higher incomes, the efficient firms attract the capital, the well-made and the cheap outsell the shoddy and the dear, generally speaking. The government may increase the efficiency of the economy by using taxes to increase the market forces which make for efficient use of scarce resources.

As a catalyst for market allocation the corporation tax is an important failure on three counts.

Firstly, it is clear that the relationship between company saving and growth is not a simple one. Statistical studies, notably by Little (1962) and Rayner and Little (1966), have failed to establish any connection between the rate of company saving and the growth of companies. In many cases the companies which grow the fastest pursue policies of distributing a large proportion of their funds, so enhancing the market price of their shares. They raise funds from their own cash flows or from a grateful stockmarket on favourable terms.

Secondly, corporation tax by encouraging companies to retain profits, allows fewer opportunities for market allocation.

The capital market plays a very important role in the capitalist system in helping to ensure that the scarce resources of the economy are allocated to those sectors of the economy the demand for whose products is expanding most rapidly, and to those firms which will use the resources most efficiently. The more companies are encouraged to save, the less of their investments will be financed by raising new money on the capital market. This reduces the proportion of investment decisions which are subjected to allocation by the market; the market gets fewer opportunities to choose between investment in various sectors of the economy and fewer opportunities to offer its funds to the most efficient companies.

If profits are earned and distributed to the shareholders, then the money may be allocated to any of a large number of ventures seeking funds. If, however, the profit is retained, no such choice exists. The misallocation that this can cause is illustrated in Table 12. This shows a range of investment opportunities, each involving the expenditure of one million dollars, facing two firms, A and B. Each firm has two million dollars which it intends to invest. Firm A will clearly invest in the projects showing the 50 per cent and 40 per cent returns on capital employment, while firm B will invest in the projects showing returns of 5 per cent and 10 per cent. Now, had their four million dollars been returned, the shareholders might have offered to finance all four of firm A's projects but none of firm B's projects. In such a case the shareholders would get a higher return on their money and the economy would be using its scarce resources to better advantage.

Table 12
Rate of Return

	Firm A	Firm B
Project		
1	50%	10%
2	40%	5%
3	30%	$2\frac{1}{2}$%
4	20%	0%

While it is legitimate to wonder whether perhaps the share-holders will not just spend their dividends if they are returned, reducing total investment, the fact remains that there are losses associated with encouraging firms to retain profits with which they can isolate themselves from the allocative influence of the capital market. Firms whose returns on capital are very low or negative are normally denied new funds by the capital market. But if profits have been retained from past periods of prosperity, these inefficient firms may continue to use the country's resources. They may finance inefficient operations and even long series of losses out of past profits. The transfer of resources would be the quicker if profit retentions were discouraged by taxation, so that when firms became out-dated they would have to go out of business and give up their scarce land, labour and capital to the new growth industries. As Edward Heath put it, we would then have the survival of the fittest (the most efficient), whereas now we have the survival of the fattest (those who had retained most of past profits).

This is the view taken by the German Government. Instead of taxing distributed profits more heavily in order to encourage company saving and so an increased *quantity* of investment, they tax retained profits more heavily in the belief that this will, by subjecting more investment to the allocative influence of the stock market, give a higher *quality* of investment.

Thirdly, corporation tax weakens the allocative influence by weakening the signals by which the market distinguishes the efficient from the inefficient uses of resources. Profits indicate to investors which are the most efficient firms and therefore the firms to invest in. Profits also indicate to firms which products to produce and which productive processes are most economical of scarce resources. A tax system which accentuated the differentials between the profitable and the unprofitable would help to steer resources into the most efficient firms and processes and into the most rapidly growing sectors of the economy. While it is true of course that a tax regime which emphasized profit differentials might encourage misallocation the other way, given that there are so many lags in the economic system, some scope for improving allocation by emphasizing profit differentials is likely to exist.

The corporation tax, however, is not a good tax from this point of view. Far from emphasizing the advantages of efficient operation and investment in expanding industries, corporation tax narrows the differentials between the successful and the unsuccessful by taxing the profitable firm heavily and the unprofitability lightly or (if they do not make any profits) not at all.

In Table 13 we compare the effects of three taxes of roughly equal yield on the profitability of an efficient company (A) and an unsuccessful company (B).

Table 13

	Company A			Company B		
	Sales tax 2%	Corp. tax 40%	Factor tax 2%	Sales tax 2%	Corp. tax 40%	Factor tax 2%
Factors at cost	100	100	102	100	100	102
Output	110	110	110	100	100	100
Gross profit	10	10	8	0	0	—2
Net profit	7·8	6	8	—2	0	—2
Tax paid	2·2	4	2	2	0	2

Both companies use 100 units of input, but A produces 10 per cent more output. The difference between the profits of the two companies before taxation is 10 units, but after the sales tax it is reduced to 9.8 units (A produces more and so pays more tax). A factor tax – a proportional tax on costs – leaves the pre-tax differentials undisturbed at 10 but a corporation tax reduces the difference to 6 units. Total tax paid by the two firms in each case is roughly 4 units. Clearly, corporation tax reduces the flow of resources from the unsuccessful to the successful company as compared to a sales tax, while on this count a factor tax gives the clearest allocation signals.

It is by no means clear for what purpose corporation income tax is levied. The idea that it is 'fair' that companies should pay taxes and so make sacrifices in proportion to their income is wildly ridiculous. The company as such does not have a nervous system and any such sacrifices are in fact made by the shareholders not the company.[1] As Turvey (1963) put it: 'It is bad enough that in Britain we extend the concept of equity to include dogs without extending it further to be "fair" to inanimate objects'. And in any case, as we saw in chapter 3, much of corporation tax is probably passed on to consumers. If, on the other hand, corporation tax is only levied because so much taxation is necessary that it must be spread over as many activities as possible in order to disguise its full extent, then we can look for more efficient methods of taxing companies.

One possibility suggested by Nevin (1963) is to change the taxation of companies so that they pay in proportion to the amount of the country's scarce resources of land, labour and capital they use instead of taxing profit. A factor tax, a proportional tax on costs, would have several advantages over the taxation of profits:

1. It would seem fairer to tax companies in proportion to the value of scarce resources they deny to the rest of the economy rather than profits which in a rough way provide an index of how efficiently the company uses these scarce resources.

2. We can see from Table 13 that a factor tax will maintain pre-tax distinctions between the rewards of the efficient and the inefficient. Indeed, in our example, where it is assumed that the taxed firms operate in a highly competitive situation where price

1. The Canadian Royal Commission on Taxation (1966) recommends treating profits as shareholders' income and taxing it as such.

is given, firm B, which was breaking even under a corporation tax and could presumably continue operating like that indefinitely, finds that with a factor tax it is now making a loss and must either become more efficient or cease to operate. In other words, a factor tax would cause some marginal units to go out of business. The proposition was advanced on page 166 that one of the factors which inhibits economic growth is the fact that inefficient firms or those in declining industries continue to hold on to resources long after the time when higher returns could have been obtained elsewhere, so that growing firms have to go short of what they require for expansion. If this is correct, then factor taxes would make an important contribution to growth by forcing some marginal units out of business. A change from corporation tax would remove the artificial stimulus given to firms to pile up reserves which may be used in future to finance marginal operation.

3. The factor-tax system would provide a great incentive to operate efficiently because inefficiency adds to costs and so adds to a factor-tax liability. This is just the opposite of what happens under the present system of company taxation in most countries. Inefficiency under a profits-tax regime reduces profits and so *reduces* the firm's tax bill. And this fact leads to a good deal of organized inefficiency which we might call waste. The building of high-prestige but low-return office blocks and the purchase of very expensive chauffeur-driven cars for executives is greatly facilitated by current practice of taxing profits heavily. With a 40 per cent profits tax such expenditure only has a final cost to the company of 60 per cent of what it appears to cost. As companies only distributed, in 1969, 66 per cent of their post-tax profits in Britain (54 per cent in the USA), the impact on the shareholders' income is further reduced. In fact, waste of this kind only costs the British shareholder 23 per cent of what it costs at sale, and the American shareholder 16·2 per cent, the rest being paid for by the government in the form of various taxes foregone and by the company itself in reduced savings. It is no wonder there is so little protest by shareholders at the wasteful use of their money.

A 3 per cent factor tax combined with the abolition of corporation tax would increase the real cost of expense-account living to British shareholders from 23·5 per cent to 40 per cent of the cash price. If, instead of reducing the company's tax liability, the new carpet in the chairman's room or the new office block in the city were to lead to an increase in taxation, these expenditures would be subjected to more careful scrutiny.

Whatever growth model is used it will be possible to use the fiscal system to make growth more likely (if the model accurately interprets the growth process). If it is believed that economies of scale are very important and that the productive units in the economy are too small to take full advantage of these scale economies, amalgamations may be encouraged by fiscal means. If the burden of company taxation were shifted in favour of licences to operate so that taxation did not vary with the scale of operation, there would be a considerable incentive for small firms to amalgamate and so reduce the taxation per unit of output. Such taxes could be set at whatever level was necessary to overcome the desire of entrepreneurs to remain independent.

This sort of effect is achieved by the cumulative turnover tax operated until 1968 by the Germans. This tax was levied on the total value of each firm's output. This meant that goods might be taxed many times in the course of production if there were several vertically unintegrated firms involved in their production. Great savings in tax liability were to be made by buying up one's suppliers and the firms to whom one sold one's goods. If it is believed that vertical integration is the most efficient way to organize industrial production, then the introduction of a cumulative turnover tax will, if it is large enough, induce the desired integration.

Vertical integration may, of course, be just the opposite of what is required. It may produce inefficient competition and freely exploiting monopolies. For this reason, among others, the Germans have abandoned the turnover tax for a tax on value added only.

Conclusions

The ways in which attempts can be made to increase the size of income through fiscal policy are very numerous. Those described here as giving impetus of a once-for-all kind offer little in the way of increased income over the long period, and from this point of view are less important. Redistribution of demand between products and regions will give only small benefits to the size of the GNP and may very well lead to its long-term reduction by opposing market forces. Regional and other programs of this nature will be undertaken primarily in response to other social objectives rather than growth of the GNP. No doubt, opportunities for subsidizing firms with falling average costs at the expense of those with rising average costs will arise and should be taken, and spectacular gains in income can be achieved when unemployed resources mean that fiscal reflation is possible. But the really big gains are to be achieved through measures which would permanently accelerate the rate of growth.

More attention could be paid to considering taxes in respect of their abilities to penalize inefficiency and reward efficiency. The extreme offence of corporation tax under this head is only one case where taxes seem ill-fitted to growth promotion. An improvement could be expected if a move towards the taxation of factors were undertaken.

Appendix : American experience

The mid-1960s saw a period of very rapid and sustained economic growth in the United States and this was largely the result of deliberate government action. The initial impetus for this expansion was given by a relaxation of monetary policy in 1963 and by the great tax cut in 1964.

The principal sources of this growth were of the once-for-all kind. Expansionary monetary and fiscal policy led to the elimination of excess capacity and a fall in unemployment rates. The growth in output was caused by narrowing the gap between actual output and the potential output of the economy.

Important steps were also taken in this period to raise the

rate of growth permanently. Measures to raise the propensity to invest were taken in 1962 with reform of the depreciation laws to accelerate the rate at which plant and machinery could be written off, and a system of investment-tax credits instituted further to subsidize investment. These measures, and the effects on business optimism of continued economic expansion, are widely held to have been effective in raising investment and so the growth rate in the 1960s. However, the inflationary pressures of 1967 led to the abandonment or modification of these investment incentives in January 1968. The administration clearly regards accelerated depreciation and investment-tax credits as a way of regulating investment over the cycle, rather than as a means of inducing a permanent rise in the propensity to invest.

Other measures undertaken by the Kennedy–Johnson administrations were consistent with a policy of government intervention to promote growth. The neighbourhood Youth Corps, Jobs Corps, and the Manpower Development and Training Act aimed at increasing useful employment rates. Medicare and Meducaid and the attack on urban problems and increased subsidization of education would produce a population more fit for productive activity. The attack on racial discrimination would increase the efficiency with which employment was allocated.

11 Summary, Conclusion and Policy Suggestions

It is with the words of Simon (1938) in mind that we approach the difficult task of rounding-off this short volume on the theory of taxation.

> It has become conventional among students of fiscal policy, however, to disemble any underlying social philosophy and to maintain a pretence of rigorous, objective analysis untinctured by mere ethical considerations. The emptiness of this pretence among economists is notorious; yet people who cannot solve a simultaneous equation still regard 'unscientific' as the ultimate in critical invective and themselves live in constant terror of that characteristic. Having been told that sentiments are contraband in the realm of science, they religiously eschew a few prescribed phrases, clutter up title pages and introductory chapters with pious references to the science of public finance, and then write monumental discourses upon their own prejudices and preconceptions (Simon, 1938, p. 97).

In this volume we discussed, in chapter 3 efficiency criteria which might be used in assessing the relative merits of the various fiscal alternatives open to governments. Then in chapters 6 to 10 we looked at five possible approaches to the general philosophy underlying the choice of tax base – the five 'approaches'. Three tasks remain. Firstly, we must make a choice of approach; secondly, we must set up a system of assessing taxes by taking account of the score of each tax on each efficiency criterion. And thirdly, we will conclude with a section laying down guidelines for tax reform.

The choice of approach

Revenue minimization (see chapter 6)

The approach of using taxes which have the highest expenditure restraining effect so as to produce full employment and price stability, given the level of expenditure, with the smallest possible revenue, seems attractive at first hearing. It would appear to be desirable that the government should minimize its revenue if it can do so without prejudicing its expenditure. And as we have seen in chapter 6, governments can do this.

However, when one looks more closely at revenue minimization, it is clear that it must be rejected as a general philosophy of taxation, for two main reasons:

1. The taxes which have the highest economic efficiency are those which fall upon the poor. The regime implied by revenue minimization would be unacceptably regressive – it would involve gross offence against most people's ideas about equity.

2. Revenue minimization would imply a continuous rise in the National Debt as budget deficits were financed by borrowing or printing money. This implies the creation of an ever-increasing stock of wealth which under a revenue-minimization regime would be financed by taxes whose incidence was chiefly on the poor. Apart from the effects over time on the distribution of income between rich and poor, there would be important effects on the future distribution of income as between work and wealth. An increasing national debt implies a greater and greater proportion of national income going in 'unearned' income and less in income from employment or enterprise. Despite the slight evidence, it seems likely that this would have disincentive effects.

This is not to say that economic efficiency is not important. It is vital that the government know the impact of taxes on private expenditure if they are going to achieve the equality, $D_p + D_g = Y_{fe}$, with precision. While *high* economic efficiency cannot be made the basis for choice between taxes, *knowledge* of the economic efficiency of taxes is an important aspect of certainty. *High* economic efficiency is rejected as an approach, but *certain* economic efficiency is an important efficiency criterion.

implies making someone better-off by making someone else worse-off. Hochman and Rogers make utility a function not only of own income but of other people's income:

$$U_M = f_M(Y_M, Y_J),$$

where U_M is Mutt's utility, and Y_M and Y_J are Mutt's and Jeff's incomes respectively. In such a case it may make the rich man feel better to have some income taken from him and given to the poor: when the rich man's own income adds less to his utility than the poor man's income adds to the rich man's utility, or when the marginal utility of $Y_J > Y_M$ in Mutt's utility equation. To the extent that utility functions are interdependent in this way, redistribution can be brought into a Paretian system. Redistribution can make both rich and poor better off.

Two points emerge from the Hochman and Rogers analysis. Firstly, the differences between the policy implications of the benefit and ability-to-pay approaches become blurred since those who are able to pay also benefit. Secondly, their analysis explains the willingness of rich people to provide themselves with private health and education services and pay for socialized services which they do not consume. In effect, they use the State to provide themselves with a vicarious increase in their own welfare.

Ingenious as the Hochman and Rogers thesis is, it can only deal with part of the problem. There are people who would rather not contribute to the support of the poor and it seems very likely that redistribution determined by such humanitarianism consumer sovereignty would fall very far short of equality. Indeed, if redistribution is just carried to the extent that the rich derive more satisfaction out of giving away their incomes than consuming them themselves, there is no reason to expect redistribution to be greater than it would be under a system of private charity – a bleak prospect.

Sismondi's (see Musgrave, 1959, p. 65) idea that a benefit approach would require the rich to pay more tax than the poor in order to buy the acquiescence of the poor in unequal distribution of income pre-dates Hochman and Rogers and may be just as useful. Without redistribution by the government, the poor would revolt. And this would be greatly to the detriment of the rich. The rich benefit from the stability which redistribution brings to the society that allows them to be rich. Looked at in this way, the benefit to the rich of redistributive taxes is the difference between personal income and the mean income for the population as a whole. The question remains of how much progression, if any, is indicated by such an analysis. The minimum of redistributive taxes that could be justified in this way is the amount that would just preserve the stability of society. But we cannot say *a priori* how much that is. As long as one man has less than an equal share, he has an incentive to try to overthrow the regime. The maximum that could be charged without taking away all of the benefits accruing to the rich would be taken by a regime which all but levelled down incomes. The second differs infinitesimally from the regime indicated by the cardinal utility ability-to-pay approach of chapter 9. However, a Paretian system of redistribution whereby no change is justified unless both parties to it are made better off, would almost certainly produce a good deal less than equality. The rich would be willing to accept some risk in order to preserve inequality.

It is possible, therefore, to come to the same sort of policy conclusions by either the 'benefit' or the 'ability' argument. The rich paying more than the poor is clearly indicated by both approaches. Progression is likely under both approaches, and levelling down of post tax incomes may even find support by either line of reasoning.

The philosophy of this writer is, like that of the Canadian Royal Commission on Taxation (1966), basically one of ability. The failure to find an ethical justification for income inequality suggests an ideal policy of levelling down of incomes. But at the same time acknowledgement must be made of the importance of simultaneous determination. One must not lose sight of the fact that taxes (however levied) are the costs of government expenditures. And government expenditure is not justified after that point where the unpleasantness of taxation exceeds the benefits of that government expenditure. The size of the public sector is determined by an assessment of costs and benefits, though the costs and benefits may to some extent be borne by different people.

This point is illustrated in Figure 33 in which Musgrave's (1959) equilibrium budget shows the benefits of ideally spent government expenditure and the disutility of optimally levied taxes. Expenditure OE is preferred when the marginal benefits are equal to the marginal disutility of taxes. Some union of the ability and benefit approach is possible over the question of income redistribution through taxation, but ability is the preferred principle. However, the advantages of market-type simultaneous determination may be taken by operating pure benefit regimes in those areas of government expenditure where no major issues of distribution or externality exist. Socialists and liberals will argue on the basis of this value judgement about how often this opportunity occurs, but the present author would expect widespread agreement that transport affords many opportunities for the application of benefit principles. A cheap system of road pricing offers many advantages in increased efficiency (see Chapter 8).

Our fifth approach was that of promoting growth, i.e. the income maximization approach. Two points should be made here. The first is that there may be costs involved in growth: people may have to take less leisure or give up some important freedoms in order to increase growth. Indeed, a sensible society would seek to *optimize* growth, not *maximize* it. The second point is that one of the costs of growth is likely to be a weakening of the ability-to-pay approach to taxation. Unless someone tries such a regime, we never can obtain proof that a tax system which levelled down incomes would inhibit growth. Nevertheless the evidence on top tax-rate payers (see for example Sanders, 1951) does suggest that weakening of incentives does take place at very high marginal rates of tax. And intuitively, it seems obvious that a capitalist society without any after-tax income differentials would not grow; indeed, it would shrink. In other words, there are levels of taxation at which a trade-off between redistribution and growth exists. Because of the power of compound interest, to solve the questions of poverty it does not seem likely that political economists would be prepared to sacrifice more than say half of the possible growth rate in the interests of redistribution. Of course, how progressive a tax regime is thereby implied will await more certain empirical evidence on taxation and incentives.

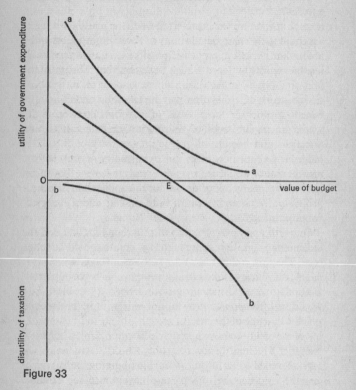

Figure 33

A synthetic approach is suggested here. It is basically an ability-to-pay approach constrained by the need to maintain incentives in the interests of growth. Measures would also be taken to reorganize taxation so as to stimulate growth by penalizing inefficiency and by subsidizing growth – promoting activity. Where it was not incompatible with redistribution policies, benefit regimes would be employed, and the total size of the government sector would be determined by an aggregative comparison of the tax costs and the benefits of such expenditures.

Assessment of efficiency

So much for the approaches. What of the efficiency criteria? (See chapter 3.) These criteria are not always compatible with one another. (For example vertical equity may not be possible if there is neutrality.) There may not be general agreement as to the desirability of some criteria (those who want to socialize the economy will favour taxes with low economic efficiencies); and then there is the problem of finding a common denominator to which the score of each tax on each criterion can be reduced for purposes of comparison.

Shoup (1969) has provided a convenient terminology which we can adapt to analyse these efficiency criteria. *Concensus criteria* are those whose validity is likely to be generally agreed. *Conflict criteria* are those which will appeal to certain interest groups but not to others.

We start by considering the concensus criteria. There can be no dispute about administrative efficiency and evasion. (We can ignore without apology the conflict with those skillful at evasion.) The other aspects of certainty (incidence, marksmanship and knowledge of, as distinct from extent of, expenditure-restraining-effect) raise no issues of conflict, and horizontal equity is an unchallenged principle.

Vertical equity is a concept which leads to conflict in interpretation. The appropriate degree of inequity with which to treat unequals is clearly open to interpretation by various interest groups. Paternalistic governments will see evident taxes as a hindrance to the expansion of the public sector whereas liberals will think evidence important as a step towards consumer sovereignty. Interventionists will want to use non-neutral taxes to alter consumption patterns. Socialists will favour taxes with low economic efficiencies which will allow repayment of the national debt.

How, then, do we choose between taxes each of which has a different score under each of the efficiency criteria? It would be convenient if we could easily reduce each rating to a money equivalent and then simply choose the most valuable – or least costly – tax. Unfortunately, only administrative efficiency is readily dealt with in money terms. Believers in neutrality might assess excess burdens in money terms, but after that the problem becomes more difficult.

The first step in producing a common denominator for these various attributes of taxes is to list them in order of importance. This is a matter of value judgement and will vary from person to person. For the sake of illustration, however, Table 14 lists a hypothetical ordering of two individuals. *A* may be described as a right-wing liberal while *B* is a left-wing socialistic paternalist.

Table 14

	A	*B*
High weighting	Horizontal equity Vertical equity Neutrality Evidence Economic efficiency (high)	Horizontal equity Vertical equity Evasion Economic efficiency (known) Certainty of incidence
Low weighting	Evasion Economic efficiency (known) Certainty of incidence Fiscal marksmanship	Fiscal marksmanship Neutrality Evidence Economic efficiency (high)

With one exception, vertical equity, which will be interpreted differently by *A* and *B*, the scores of each tax under each heading are matters of fact (though the facts may not be known). In order to assess taxes, *A* and *B* will attach weights to each efficiency criterion. Note that *B* will attach a negative weight to evidence and economic efficiency, and perhaps to neutrality.

There is a great deal of work for the economist to do in describing the facts about these efficiency criteria. But it is up to the politicians to attach weights on the basis of their value judgement, their assessment of the public will or their guesses about which tax regime will produce the happiest community.

The optimal budget

We can return to Figure 33 and define an optimal budget. It is the job of government (a) to spend money so as to produce as many benefits as possible – to push *aa* out to the right; and (b) to tax as efficiently as possible so as to move *bb* out to the right also. An optimal budget therefore is one which maximizes OE.

A rational budget

Perhaps the most disappointing aspect of the theory of taxation is that it is possible to know it all without knowing what to do about the tax systems with which countries find themselves, which nearly everyone agrees are in some ways unsatisfactory. However, there are practical lessons to be learned from a study of such matters, and by far the most important is that a country should have both a clearly defined set of tax objectives and methods with which to achieve these objectives effectively.

The tax systems of Britain and the United States have grown up piece-meal. As the objectives of taxation changed through time, new taxes were added but old taxes were seldom abolished. Our tax regimes have grown up through the operations of pre-Keynesian Chancellors of the Exchequer who were looking for the least unpopular method of raising sufficient revenue to cover government expenditure. The system has been added to by Keynesian Chancellors aiming to fulfil first of all the very different objective of reducing consumption by just the right amount to allow the governments to make their expenditures without causing inflation. While this remains the basic objective of taxation, there is no doubt that the emphasis of economic management is now firmly aimed at promoting growth. Growth-promoting measures are added to the existing structure of tax rates. No comprehensive reappraisal of the tax system in terms of the current policy objectives is undertaken.

As Turvey (1963) put it, the (British) tax system is not goal orientated but is an evolutional monument.

It is unlikely, if we could start from scratch, that we would choose the present systems of taxation in Britain or the USA. But this is not quite a good enough reason to justify a complete overhaul of the tax system – to meet an ideal. The disruption that would be caused by sudden and radical tax changes might well be too high a price to pay for a saner tax system. However, that is not to say that there should not be such a clearly defined tax system towards which fiscal changes are gradually modified. One country which has decided to adopt such a policy is Canada (see the Royal Commission on Taxation, 1966).

Such a model tax regime would be one in which the objectives of taxation were clearly specified and all taxes directed towards one or several of these objectives. No taxes would be imposed unless they were clearly seen to be able to contribute to the fulfillment of such policy objectives. One such model tax system is outlined below. No suggestion is made that this is the only model, and no exact indication of the relative intensity of such taxes is given.

As we saw in Chapter 1, the basic reason for taxation is the need to control private expenditure or to allow the government to use scarce resources without causing inflation. But we have rejected efficiency in so reducing private expenditure as a general basis for choice. Ultimately, taxes will be chosen on the foundation of how well they are consistent with other objectives of government policies. Let us take as the main objectives redistribution of economic power, reduction in the consumption of demerit goods, and growth and stabilization.

Objective 1

The first objective is the evening out of the grosser inequalities of economic power produced by the market economy. The current tax systems in Britain and the United States really make a rather inefficient job of reducing inequalities of economic power. They tax money income very progressively indeed and also tax capital gains. But there is no taxation at all of wealth apart from a highly avoidable death duty. This is an unfortunate state of affairs on at least three counts:

1. It does not tax all of what constitutes riches. It is possible to be very rich indeed, but so to organize your affairs as to make little or no taxable income and live royally off your capital.

2. It stops people *becoming* rich, by taxing the earnings by which accumulation of capital takes place while it does nothing to stop people *being* rich. This leads to an ossification of the wealth structure of society. Part, at least, of the opposition to extreme wealth would disappear if in fact everyone had an equal chance of becoming rich. What is so unfair about this great concentration of redistributive taxes on current incomes and the exemption of capital assets is that, apart from a very few exceptions, one must be born to wealth to stand any real chance of enjoying it.

3. This ossification of the distribution of wealth may have un-desirable implications for growth because (a) the very rich do not have to protect their assets by making them profitable enough to pay wealth taxes and (b) it is so difficult to *become* rich that fewer people may try.

The policy suggestion therefore is a change in the emphasis of redistribution policy from income to wealth. Two cautionary notes must be made. Firstly, there is a limit to how much can be done in this respect by one country alone. If capital is heavily taxed in one country it is very likely to emigrate to another country where it is more favourably treated. Unless all major countries followed suit, it is hard to envisage a successful wealth tax whose top rate was much above 1 per cent per annum. Secondly, the economic efficiency of the wealth tax is likely to be very low indeed, so that little scope exists for replacing the lower income-tax rates by such a tax. What we are considering here is the replacement of the top rates of income taxes (which also have very low economic efficiencies) by a wealth tax. This would make it easier to become rich and more difficult to stay rich.

Objective 2

For whatever the reasons, all people in their political roles seem to want a faster rate of growth than their unfettered and sovereign economic activities would produce. The promotion of faster economic growth may be pursued in two ways: (a) the budget should continue to foster growth by promoting investment by subsidies; and (b) growth should be promoted by increasing the ability of the market to allocate scarce resources to the most efficient firms and to the growing sectors of industry. This would involve abolishing corporate income tax, and replacing it by a factor tax. This would increase the rewards of efficiency and increase the penalties for using scarce resources inefficiently. The consequences of waste would thus be magnified by taxation, whereas under corporation tax regimes these consequences are reduced. This would encourage the flow of capital into the most productive enterprises.

The allocative influence of the stock and money markets is greatly weakened by the insulation of many companies from such influence by the existence of retained profits. In order to force more firms to seek funds in the open market, it is proposed that while corporation tax be done away with a vestigial corporation tax remain and be levied on retained profits only. This would discriminate, as in Germany, in favour of the distribution of profits. More firms would thus have to go on the basis of their past records to the stock and money markets and only those with good records and/or good prospects would receive finance. The inefficient would be pushed more quickly out of business.

What of the effective incidence of such a tax reform? Will this not involve a shift in the burden of taxation from profit owners to consumers, i.e. will it not be a highly regressive measure? It all depends on the extent to which corporation taxes are shifted (see p. 60). If there is total shifting, then there are no important distributional effects of this tax reform. If zero shifting takes place, a rise in retail prices of the order of 2 per cent might be expected. As the truth lies somewhere between zero and 100 per cent shifting, such a price would probably be well worth paying.

Objective 3

The third objective is that of distorting consumer choices by taxes or subsidies (a) because there are external costs or benefits which the market does not take into account, or (b) because people are ignorant of their long-run preferences and so take sub-optimal decisions on short-run considerations, or (c) because society believes the consumption of some good is in some absolute sense undesirable. To fulfil these objectives specific taxes such as excise duties or purchase taxes are required.

It is important to note that the neutrality approach to taxation is being defied directly here. The presumption is that the benefits of altering consumption of such goods and services exceeds any excess burden resulting from the distortion of choices.

Objective 4

The fourth objective is that of compensatory fiscal policy – the inducement of marginal changes in private consumption so as to maintain the balance between the ability of the economy to produce goods and services and the private and public demands for these goods and services.

A rough equality of $D_g + D_p$ and Y_{fe} will be maintained by taking forecasts of the growth of potential output and private spending propensities along with planned government expenditures, and setting the various taxes which we have proposed at levels which, if the forecasts and plans are realised, will induce balance in the economy, that is, full employment without inflation.

However, from time to time, and perhaps quite often, these plans will go wrong, either because the model was wrong or because of exogenous shocks to the system such as international monetary crises, national disasters or wars. This may necessitate slight and perhaps temporary changes in tax rates to maintain stability.

On such occasions, when marginal adjustments to taxes are required, it is not necessary to raise all taxes. In fact, as a very delicate operation is being undertaken and as a very certain result is required, a tax with special qualities is called for. The qualities necessary are speed of implementation and impact, not one with long lags; a predictable yield, not one in which marksmanship is erratic; and high economic efficiency. Since what is required is a reduction in consumption, other taxes which have other objectives should be interfered with as little as possible. General taxes on consumption perform well on all these counts. Retail sales taxes, taxes on value added, or factor taxes are suggested.

We have already included in our model tax system a factor tax, so it may be given the sole job of performing short-run stabilization tasks. If it were found that there were longer lags associated with factor-tax changes, a retail sales tax might be added to the fiscal armoury with the specific task of stabilizing demand by being raised or lowered.

All other taxes would be scrapped, and changes would be undertaken by altering the rates of the tax to suit the policy objective. We would not have, as the British had in 1967, the spectacle of an inflationary situation being tackled by what was in effect a tax on capital which was not expected to have any impact on expenditure whatsoever.

References

ACKLEY, G. (1961), *Macroeconomic Theory*, Macmillan.

ALLAN, C. M. (1965), 'Fiscal marksmanship', *Oxford Economic Papers*, vol. 17, no. 2, pp. 317–28.

ALTMAN, S. H., and FECHTER, A. E. (1967), 'The supply of military manpower in the absence of the draft', *Amer. Econ. Rev.*, vol. 57, no. 2, pp. 19–31.

ARROW, K. J. (1962), 'The economic implications of learning by doing', *Rev. econ. Studies*, vol. 29, no. 80, pp. 155–73.

ARROW, K. J. (1963), *Social Choice and Individual Values*, Wiley.

BOWEN, H. R. (1948), *Toward Social Economy*, Holt, Rinehart & Winston.

BRACEWELL–MILNES, W. (1967), 'The concept of intension: a new approach to the "progressiveness" of taxes', *Pub. Finance*, pp. 520–28.

BROWN, C. V., and DAWSON, D. A. (1969), *Personal Taxation, Incentives and Tax Reform*, Political and Economic Planning.

BUCHANAN, J. M. (1966), '*Inconsistencies in the National Health Service*', Institute of Economic Affairs, Occasional Paper No. 7.

Canadian Royal Commission on Taxation, 1966.

CRAGG, J. G., HARBERGER, A. C., and MEISZKOWSKI, P. (1967), 'Empirical evidence on the incidence of the corporation income tax', *J. polit. Econ.*, vol. 75, no. 5, pp. 811–21.

DOW, J. C. R. (1964), *The Management of the British Economy*, National Institute of Social and Economic Research.

DUESENBERRY, J. (1949), *Income, Saving and the Theory of Consumer Behavior*, Harvard University Press.

FISHER, A. C. (1969), 'The cost of the draft and the cost of ending the draft', *Amer. Econ. Rev.*, vol. 59, no. 3, pp. 239–54.

FRIEDMAN, M. (1952), 'The welfare effects of an income and an excise tax', *J. polit. Econ.*, vol. 60, no. 1, pp. 1–24.

FRIEDMAN, M., and FRIEDMAN, R. D. (1962), *Capitalism and Freedom*, University of Chicago Press.

GEORGESCU–ROEGAN, N. (1954), 'Choice expectations and measurability', *Q. J. Econ.*, vol. 68, no. 4, pp. 503–32.

GEORGESCU–ROEGAN, N. (1966), *Analytical Economics*, Harvard University Press.

GORDON, R. J. (1967), 'The incidence of corporation tax', *Amer. Econ. Rev.*, vol. 57, no. 4, pp. 731–58.

HALL, R. L., and HITCH, C. J. (1939), 'Price theory and business behaviour', *Oxford Econ. Papers*, vol. 2, no. 2, pp. 12–45.

HARSANYI, J. C. (1955), 'Cardinal welfare, individualistic ethics and interpersonal comparisons of utility', *J. polit. Econ.*, vol. 63, no. 4, pp. 309–21.

HICKS, J. R. (1939), *Value and Capital*, Oxford University Press.

HICKS, U. K. (1946), 'The terminology of tax analysis', *Econ. J.*, vol. 56, no. 221, pp. 38–50.

HICKS, U. K. (1947), *Public Finance*, Cambridge University Press.

HOCHMAN, H. M., and ROGERS, J. D. (1969), 'Pareto-optimal redistribution', *Amer. Econ. Rev.*, vol. 59, no. 4, pp. 542–7.

JOHANSON, L. (1963), 'Some notes on the Lindahl theory of public expenditure', *International econ. Rev.*, vol. 4, no. 3, pp. 346–58.

JOSEPH, M. W. F. (1939), 'The excess burden of indirect taxation', *Rev. Econ. Studies*, vol. 6, no. 3, pp. 226–31.

KALDOR, N. (1956), *An Expenditure Tax*, Allen & Unwin.

KEYNES, J. M. (1936), *The General Theory of Employment, Interest and Money*, Macmillan.

KEYNES, J. M. (1940), *How to Pay for the War*, Macmillan.

KRZYANIAK, M., and MUSGRAVE, R. A. (1963), *The Shifting Incidence of Corporation Income Tax*, Johns Hopkins Press.

LAUMAS, G. S. (1966), 'The shifting of corporation income tax: a study with reference to Indian corporations', *Pub. Finance*, vol. 21, no. 4, pp. 462–72.

LEES, D. S. (1961), *Health Through Choice*, Hobart Paper no. 14, Institute of Economic Affairs.

LEES, D. S. (1967), 'Efficiency in government spending: social services: health', *Pub. Finance*, vol. 22, no. 1, pp. 176–89.

LINDAHL, E. (1919), 'Just taxation: a just solution', pp. 168–76, in R. A. Musgrave and A. T. Peacock (eds.), *Classics in the Theory of Public Firms*, Macmillan, 1958.

LITTLE, I. M. D. (1951), 'Direct versus indirect taxes', *Econ. J.*, vol. 61, no. 243, pp. 577–84.

LITTLE, I. M. D. (1962), *Higgledy Piggledy Growth*, Bulletin of the Oxford Institute of Statistics.

MCGUIRE, M. C., and AARON, H. (1969), 'Efficiency and equity in the optimal supply of a public good', *Rev. Econ. Stat.*, vol. 51, no. 1, pp. 31–9.

MARSHALL, A. (1890), *Principles of Economics*, Macmillan.

MEADE, J. E. (1964), *Efficiency, Equality and the Ownership of Property*, Allen & Unwin.

MERRETT, A. J. (1965), 'The capital gains tax', *Lloyds Bank Rev.* no. 78, pp. 1–14.

MOORE, M. (1968), 'Progressive taxation revisited', *Pub. Finance*, vol. 23, no. 3, pp. 246–67.

MORAG, A. (1959), 'Is the economic efficiency of taxation important', *Econ. J.*, vol. 69, no. 273, pp. 87–94.

MUSGRAVE, R. A. (1959), *The Theory of Public Finance*, McGraw-Hill.

MUSGRAVE, R. A. (1966), 'Provision for social goods', in J. Margolis and H. Guitton (eds.), *Public Economics*, International Economic Association.

MUSGRAVE, R. A. (1969), *Fiscal Systems*, Yale University Press.

NEVIN, E. (1963), Taxation for growth: a factor tax, *Westminster Bank Rev.*, November, pp. 13–25.

PEACOCK, A. T., and WISEMAN, J. (1964), *Education for Democrats*, Institute of Economics, Hobart Paper No. 25.

PIGOU, A. C. (1912), *Study in Public Finance*, Macmillan.

RAYNER, A. C., and LITTLE, I. M. D. (1966), *Higgledy Piggledy Growth Again*, Blackwell.

REY, M. (1965), 'Estimating tax evasions: the example of the Italian general sales tax', *Pub. Finance*, vol. 20, no. 3, pp. 366–86.

ROBBINS, L. (1932), *An Essay on the Nature and Significance of Economic Science*, Macmillan.

ROBBINS, L. (1947), *The Economic Problem in Peace and War*, Macmillan.

ROBBINS, L. (1964), *Higher Education*, Cmnd. 2145, V. HMSO.

ROSKAMP, K. W. (1965), 'The shifting of taxes on business income: the case of West German corporation', *National Tax J.*, vol. 18, no. 3, pp. 247–57.

ROTH, J. G. (1966), 'A self financing road system', Institute of Economic Affairs, Research Monograph, No. 3.

SAMUELSON, P. A. (1954), 'The pure theory of public expenditure', *Rev. Econ. Stat.*, vol. 36, no. 4, pp. 387–9.

SAMUELSON, P. A. (1955), 'Diagramatic exposition of a theory of public expenditure', *Rev. Econ. Stat.*, vol. 37, no. 4, pp. 350–56.

SAMUELSON, P. A. (1958), 'Aspects of public expenditure theories', *Rev. Econ. Stat.*, vol. 40, no. 4, pp. 332–6.

SAMUELSON, P. A. (1969), 'Contrast between welfare conditions for joint supply and for public goods', *Rev. Econ. Stat.*, vol. 51, no. 1, pp. 26–30.

SANDERS, T. H. (1951), *Effects of taxation on executives*, Harvard Graduate School of Business Administration.

SELDON, A. (1967), *Taxation and Welfare*, Institute of Economic Affairs Research, Monograph, No. 14.

SELIGMAN, E. R. A. (1958), *Introduction to the Shifting and Incidence of Taxation* in R. A. Musgrave and C. S. Shoup, Readings in the Economics of Taxation, American Economic Association.

SHOUP, C. S. (1969), *Public Finance*, Weidenfeld & Nicolson.
SIMON, H. C. (1938), *Personal Income Taxation*, Chicago University Press.
SMITH, A. (1776), *The Wealth of Nations*, Dent.
TURVEY, R. (1963), 'A tax system without company taxation', *Lloyds Bank Rev.*, no. 67, pp. 30–44.
TURVEY, R. (1968), *Public Enterprise*, Penguin.

Acknowledgements

I would like to thank Miss D. A. Dawson of the University of Glasgow, Mr A. G. Kemp of the University of Aberdeen and Mr R. W. Houghton of the University of Sheffield for reading my manuscript. Professor K. J. W. Alexander, Mr A. B. Jack and Dr A. J. Phipps of the University of Strathclyde, Professor D. S. Lees of the University of Nottingham and Professor P. Robson of St Andrews have also read individual chapters and made suggestions for which I am grateful. Mr B. J. McCormick has been a tireless general editor. Mr Gordon Pert gave me valuable technical assistance with the diagrams. And I would like to thank Mrs Ann Wells and Miss Sandra whose ability to interpret my writing and good humour in typing successive drafts was a great help.

Having made so many acknowledgements I can hardly claim that this volume is all my own work. However as I did not take all the advice that was given I feel justified in laying exclusive claim to responsibility for the shortcomings which remain.

Index